BOQUERIA

BOQUERIA

A Cookbook, from Barcelona to New York

Marc Vidal & Yann de Rochefort

with Zack Bezunartea

A.

CONTENTS

INTRODUCTION

The Dinner Rush

It's 6:30 pm on a Thursday at Boqueria 19th Street, and the relentless buzz of the kitchen printer signals the beginning of the dinner rush. A string of tickets inches over the back of the old ink-jet printer and snakes its way across the worn butcher's block where plates are staged and garnished before being sent to the tables.

Chef Marc turns toward Oaxaco, who, just as he has every day for the last ten years, stands behind him at a small table preparing potatoes for patatas bravas. His stout fingers move on autopilot, peeling and dicing in just a couple of quick gestures.

Marc yanks the long perforated stretch of orders from the printer and holds it in the air, his arm outstretched at shoulder height. "Look at this, Oaxaco! It's taller than you." Oaxaco looks at the slim ribbon of paper, and flashes his crooked smile. "But it's way skinnier!"

The cooks laugh and Marc begins to call the tickets to them in breakneck Spanglish.

"Fire dos gambas!"

"Fire datiles, cuatro piezas!"

"Tres albondigas!"

"Fire tres espinacas, one no garlic!"

One by one, cooks yell "Oido!"—signaling to Chef that they heard the orders. Pots clank. Oven doors slam. Within minutes, the grill is full, covered with fresh squid, juicy lamb skewers, hanger steak and Ibérico pork. Flashes of fire dance over the sautée station as brandy burns off the garlicky ajillo shrimp. Basketfuls of patatas bravas and croquetas are shocked to a crackle as they hit the deep fryer. The cooks scramble to toss, dress, season, and sear, all while holding a complex puzzle of orders and cooking times in their heads.

Cooks, tongs, and plates shift and spin past each other until that old butcher block fills with the finished tapas. Marc turns toward the server station.

"Runner, please!!!"

The dining room staff rush in and Marc crosses dishes off the tickets as he directs.

"Gambas table 13 and 36."

"Four piece dates, 108."

"Espinacas, 40."

Servers grab the plates and run them into the packed dining room, holding them high in the air where they hold altitude next to the hanging Edison bulbs before landing in front of hungry guests.

Yann, the owner, stops in front of the small coat closet wedged between the bar and the dining area and watches the action.

There's a first date on table 35 that looks like it's going well, and one on 12 that doesn't. A group of co-workers on 31 just broke out into hearty laughter, and the two enviably stylish older women at the next table look on in amusement. A bartender shakes a cocktail while recounting a Barça soccer match to the regulars in front of him. They scrape up the last savory bits of rice from a paella pan and bang the spoon against their plates to loosen the sticky caramelized grains.

Yann cracks the door of the coat closet and reaches in, keeping his eyes and ears fixed on the room. He brushes the wall gently until he finds the dimmers and the volume control. The nightly party is on. It's time to dim the lights and turn up the music. This is the energy that he had seen so many times in his favorite spots in Barcelona and wanted to capture when he first envisioned Boqueria.

Much like New York, Barcelona is an eccentrically cosmopolitan city with a distinctive character. Its long history as a magnet for pioneers of design and cuisine expresses itself today in the effortless style of its citizens as they ramble down the wide promenades, passing the fairytale façades of Gaudí's masterpieces before settling into the cafés and tapas bars that anchor every neighborhood street.

These neighborhood spots are at once charged with history and charging ahead. They are lively places where neighbors and friends come together to break bread and have a couple of short glasses of ice-cold draft beer. Bartenders smile and customers shout orders over an awe-inspiring and meticulously prepared variety of tapas. Plates of just-fried golden croquettes let off steam while mounds of mushrooms wait to be sautéed. Platters filled to overflowing with every imaginable combination of salads, pâtés, vegetables, and seafood paint the bar with tempting bursts of edible color.

There is something about eating this way—sharing a variety of delicious dishes and drinks with friends—that provokes conversation. "I'll fight you for that last squid!" "Mind if I soak up the sauce?" "Wow! What's in that?"

Talk of food inevitably turns to other topics. It is a time-honored, informal, and genuine way to connect: the original social network. That's why we always have to turn up the music a little throughout the evening, to compete with the animated conversations.

By sharing our recipes and stories with you here, we hope to give you everything you need to bring the Boqueria experience to life in your own home. Although you may never peel a potato as quickly as Oaxaco, Chef Marc has adapted our favorite dishes to be prepared with ease in your kitchen. Our recipes are as fun to shop for and to cook as they are to eat. We want to share that joy with you and your guests.

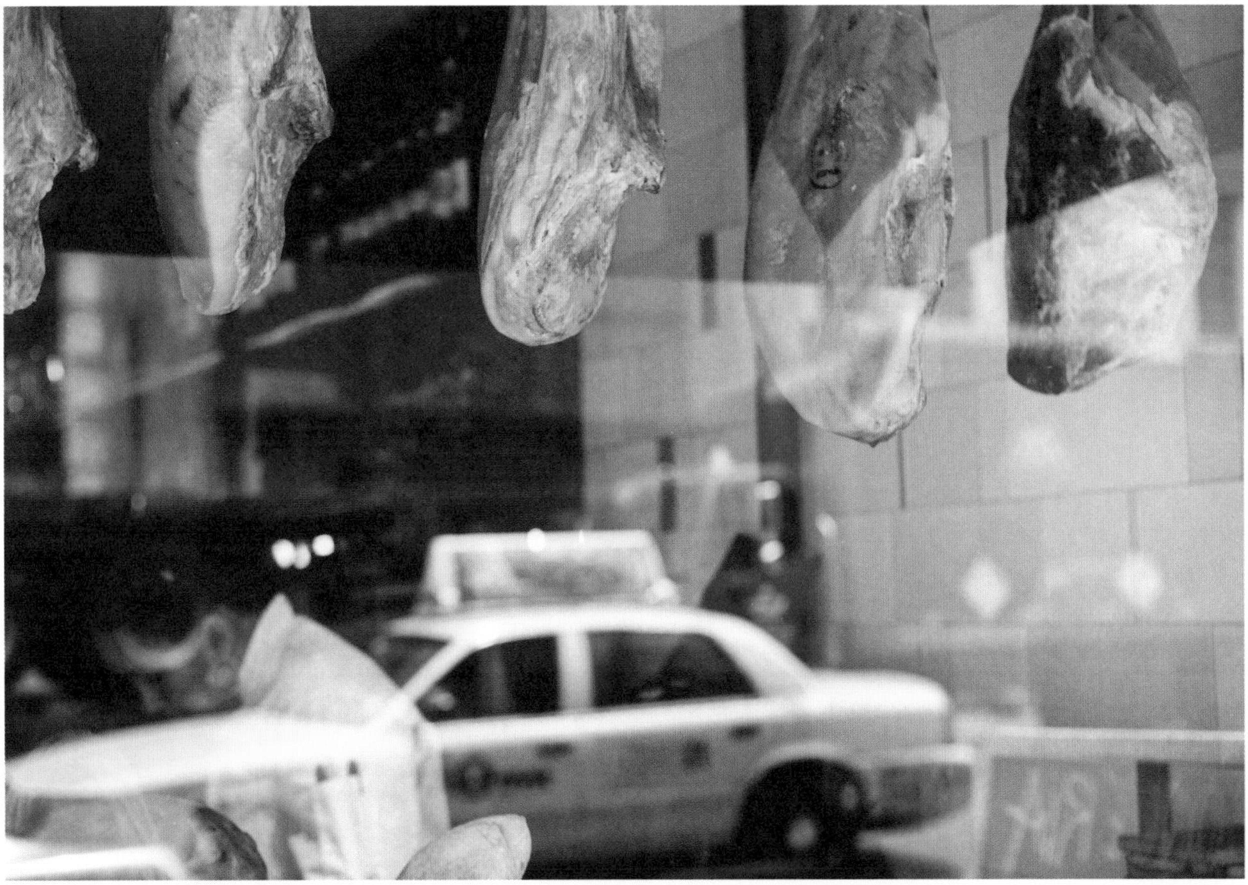

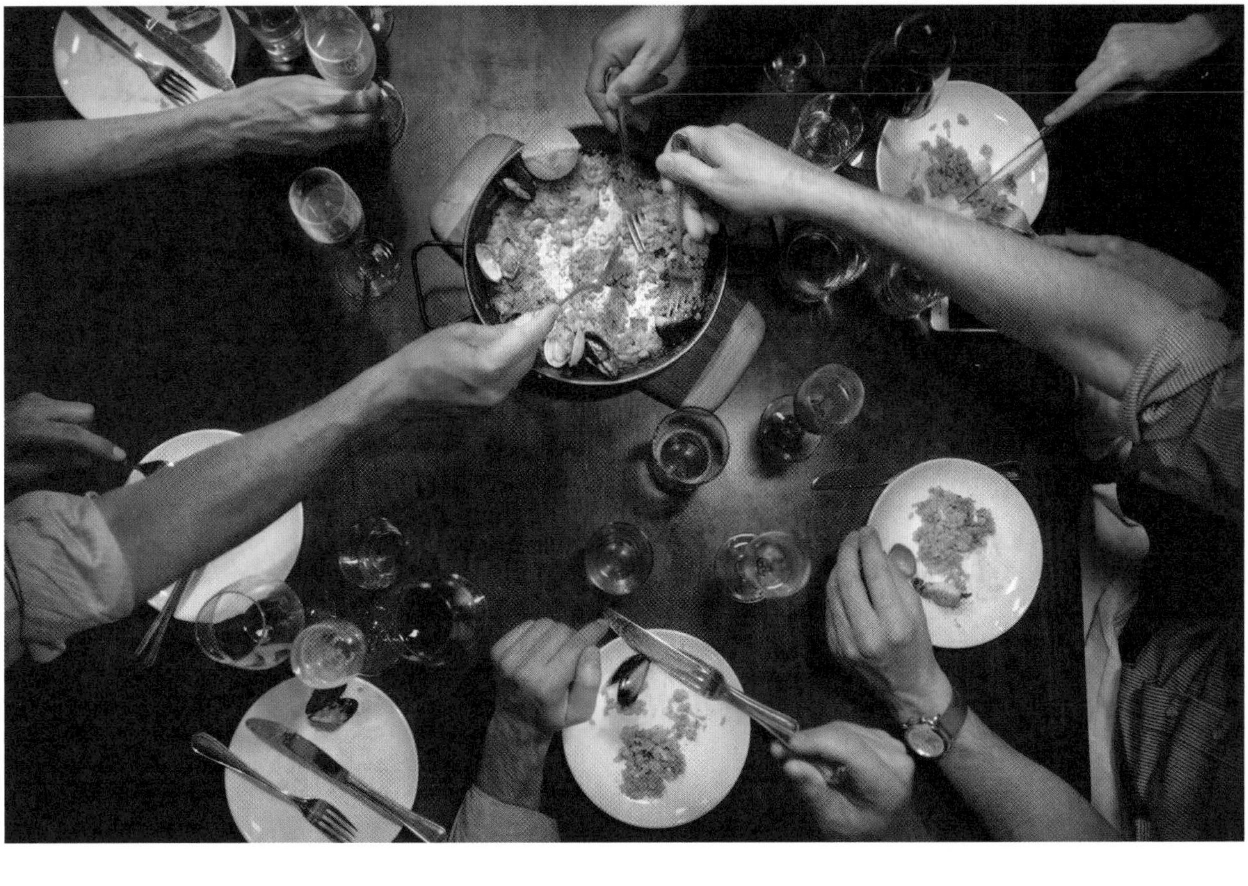

The Origins of Boqueria—Yann de Rochefort, Founder

The path to Boqueria began either ten years before our 2006 opening or 40 years before then, depending on how you look at it. Although I didn't really start thinking about opening a restaurant until 1996, my love affair with Spain started much earlier.

As a marketing executive, flying around the world for Sauza Tequila or L'Oréal shampoo, I had nursed an ambition to become an entrepreneur. That this ambition found its expression as a restaurateur was almost by chance. While living in New York City in the 1990s, I hatched a plan with some friends to open a bar—the sort of plan you make over (many) drinks and that is soon forgotten. Though, for some reason, I didn't forget it.

I kept thinking about it, dreaming up ideas, looking for partners, and scouting potential venues. In the end, I was seduced by an abandoned restaurant project on the Lower East Side. Someone had spent years excavating a basement on Ludlow St. to create a magical, subterranean "grotto," and it was my good fortune to find it.

Since it was too big for just a bar, I thought, "Why not open a restaurant?" I had never run a restaurant, and my only prior hospitality experience had ended with me getting fired from a college server gig after just two days. What could go wrong?

Nevertheless, I worked on the project nights and weekends, and somehow managed to raise enough money to claim that basement space on the Lower East Side. I juggled my day job at Allied Domecq, the world's second-largest wine and spirits company, with moonlighting as a budding restaurateur with my then business partner and still friend Phil Morgan. In 2000 we opened Suba, an expectation-defying Spanish restaurant on Ludlow St. Suba was an ambitious restaurant in a difficult location. We were in for a challenge.

Here are the facts:

- The owners of Suba had never run a restaurant.
- The dining room was in the basement and surrounded by a moat.
- The chef was French but the menu was Spanish.

None of it was exactly a recipe for success.

Despite that, Suba lasted nearly ten years and helped me get my start in the business. Boqueria would not have been possible without the years of experience I gained in that first venture.

My first restaurant taught me just how hard the business can be. Most people do not appreciate just how many different things have to go right to create the perfect guest experience. Consequently, my advice to anyone not already in this industry who dreams of opening a restaurant is this: "If you have ANY other legal means of supporting yourself, do that instead." Until you establish yourself, and even after you do, running a restaurant is hard work.

In retrospect, it still amazes me that the thought of quitting and going back to a "real job" never entered my head. Through hell and high water (and with a moat-surrounded dining room, high water was an all-too-common calamity) my stubborn streak held up. This HAD to work.

What did I take away from that first experience?

1. You should give people what they want. (As a former publicist once told me, while we were dining at an "ambitious" chef-owned restaurant, "I want to ask the chef: 'Is this your dinner, or my dinner?'")
2. Know *exactly* what you want people to think about your restaurant (think condensed "elevator pitch"—that is, one that could be expressed in a 20-second elevator ride).
3. Build a team that supports you—or abandon all hope of the semblance of a normal life.
4. When everything lines up, running a restaurant can be an intensely satisfying experience.

Long before the idea of opening a restaurant (let alone several of them) became a real project, the genesis of Boqueria had started with repeated exposure to Spanish food and culture.

Although I grew up in France, as a child I spent every August sailing in the Mediterranean with my parents. Leaving Barcelona after a few days of shopping to stock up our little boat with Rioja, whiskey, cans of anchovies, etc., we spent the month of August sailing between Ibiza, Mallorca and Menorca.

This all sounds far more glamorous than the reality: a family of five children crammed on a 35-foot sailboat helmed by a father figure with autocratic tendencies even for a boat captain. Still, it all made for great memories.

Much later, I returned to Barcelona as a 17-year-old boarding school escapee to attend a year abroad as a high school senior. Getting high on the Ramblas and dating Swedish girls from the "Spanish for Foreigners" school one flight below my abode was a *huge* step up from Deerfield, the (then) all-boys prep school I'd left behind.

A few years later, I returned to Spain again to work in Madrid for six months during my MBA internship with Colgate. This time with greater means and independence, I ventured deeper into Spanish gastronomy. Bars such as José Luis, Cibeles, and Viva Madrid intensified my love of tapas bars and planted a seed that would germinate years later. Eating like this was fun in a way that a "regular" meal never was. You could sample a range of deceptively simple yet memorable dishes and stay or leave whenever the spirit moved you; groups could form and disband at will as people joined you or moved on; and you committed to the experience one bite at a time. Eating at the bar or standing up gave these spaces an energy that most restaurants could never match.

It was this accumulated experience and web of memories that all came together in Boqueria.

When we opened Boqueria in 2006, there were generally two types of tapas place in New York: bars that provided loads of fun but little in the way of culinary ambition … and the reverse.

Boqueria was our attempt at offering all the fun of tapas bars with no compromises. All the fun (or at least most of the fun) of a dive bar, without compromising on what was on your plate.

Ten years later, it still works. Boqueria is the sort of place you can bring anyone, any group, any night. It feels both like home and like nowhere else.

Cal Pep, Barcelona, Spain

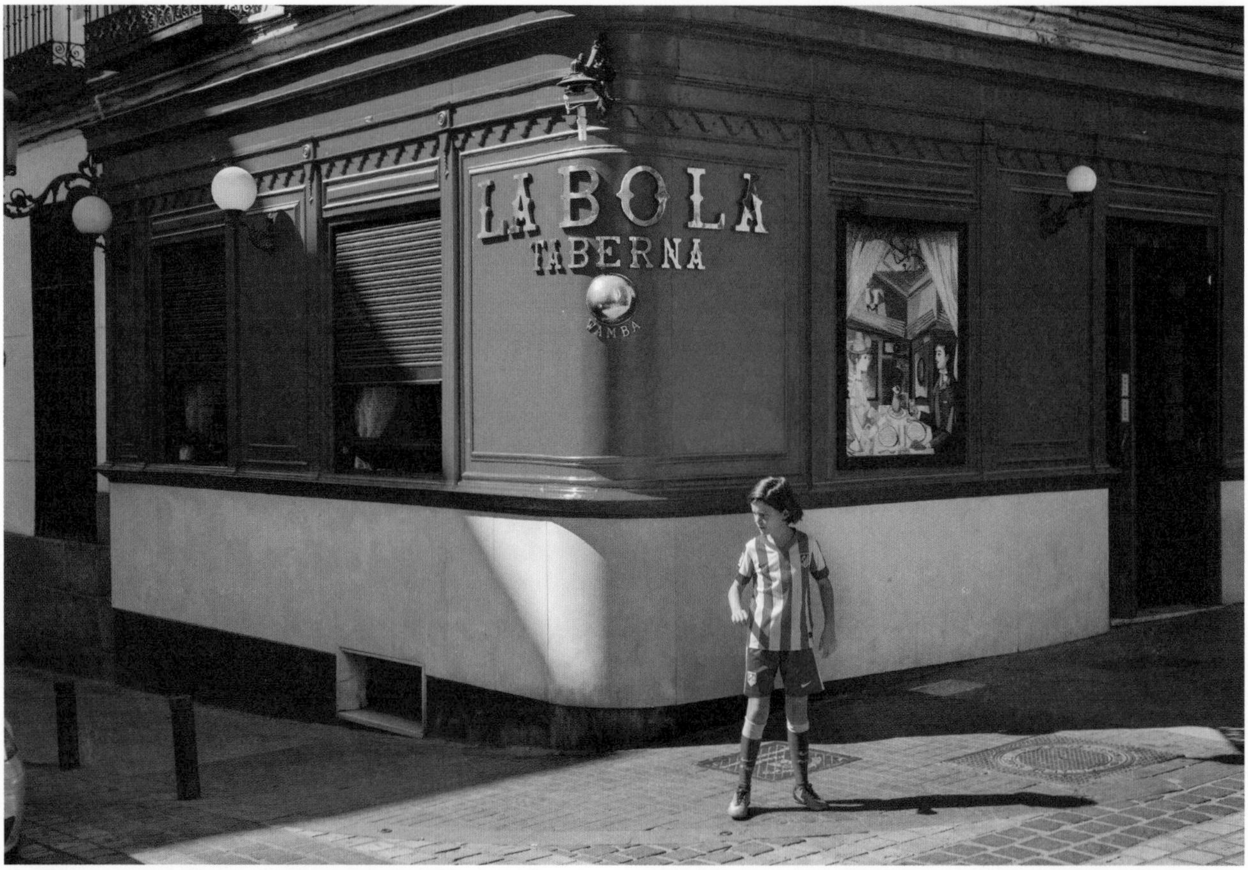
LA BOLA
TABERNA

Estrella Galicia

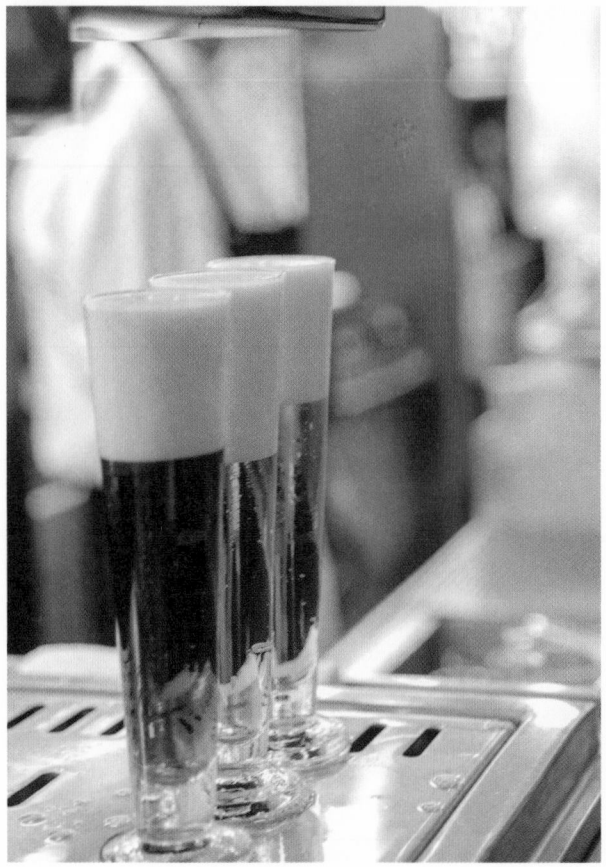

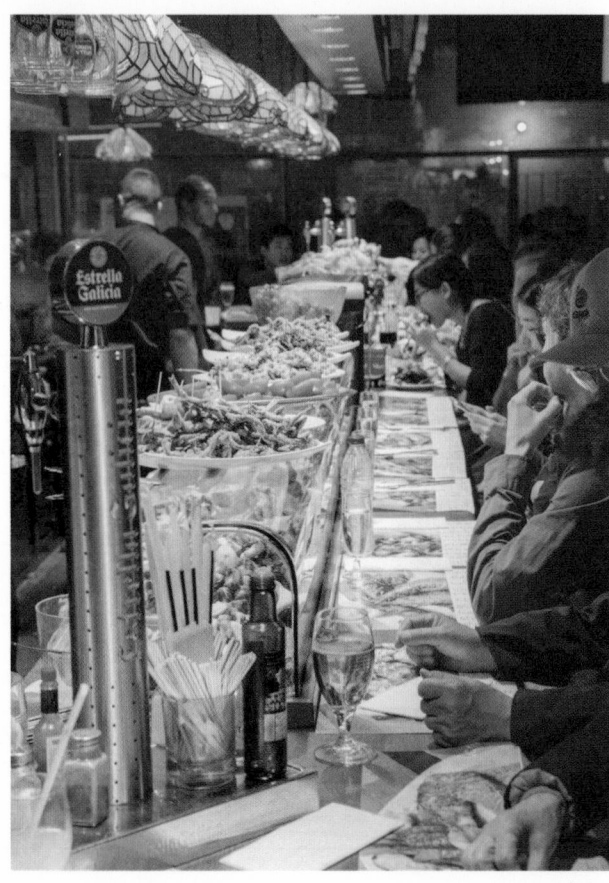

It's Beautiful

The phone was ringing but Will Meyer wasn't picking up. Will was one of the two principals of Meyer Davis, the young design studio Yann had cajoled into designing Boqueria, his second restaurant. Yann stood on 19th Street, peering into Boqueria, watching the staff polish glasses and set the tables for the first (mock) service. He dialed Will again. Still no answer.

Two years earlier, Yann had traveled to Barcelona with Will and business partner Gray Davis to start the design process. He wanted to show them his favorite haunts, hoping they could help him capture the essence of the city. He was in love with the modern design he'd seen in Barcelona and wanted Boqueria to strike this great balance between upscale and intimate. "Stark and modern" was an option, but it wouldn't have felt warm or embraced any heritage. He knew that the restaurant had to be beautiful. He loved architecture and design and wanted the restaurant to reflect that passion.

In Barcelona, design inspiration is everywhere. They visited the warm but minimalist Hotel Omm, in the fashionable El Eixample neighborhood, and ventured through the cobblestone, tree-lined streets of El Born to the must-visit restaurant El Xampanyet, where they sipped cava and gazed at the tiled walls and shelves lined with bottles of Catalan wine. At Paco Meralgo, they settled on high bar stools at a table in the tiny tapas bar and focused their attention on the cozy, modern design and the large chalkboard menu covered in carefree Catalan script.

Just before heading back to New York, Yann spotted some beautiful Catalan modern door handles in a small hardware shop and bought them on sight. They would be perfect for the front doors.

Now, he stood facing the restaurant and glanced at the handles, appreciating them anew. Although he had spent the better part of the previous eight months in the small space, it had been in construction, and this was the first time he was seeing the restaurant. The tarp that had protected the bar top during construction had been removed to reveal a heavy marble slab. The mess of tools and Masonite gone, he could finally see the polished concrete floors and the curved banquettes that hugged the dining room. The walls, clad in white oak, soaked up the golden incandescence of the simple lightbulbs. The warm glow spilled out into summer twilight. What he had been imagining for years stood right in front of him.

As the staff continued to fine-tune the dining room and prep for service, Yann dialed Will again. They had spent weeks going back and forth about tile choices, table heights, stool design, ceilings, and numerous other seemingly insignificant details that no one might ever notice but that would either add up to a beautiful, seamless experience, or trip up the vibe like a false note in an orchestra. Inevitably, there had been bumps in the road, compromises, changing minds and differences of opinions—always against the clock. Maybe that was why Will wasn't answering. He was probably thinking, "What now?"

Will finally picked up. "Yann…" The hesitation and trepidation in his voice were palpable. Yann put his fears to rest: "Will, I'm standing outside the restaurant. It's beautiful." And it really was.

Marc Vidal, Executive Chef

When I turned nine years old, my mom finally managed to put me to work at Bar Roca, the restaurant that she and her family ran. It was 1986. Ronald Reagan was on TV all the time, and Argentina (with Diego Maradona) won the World Cup. Barcelona was selected to host the '92 Olympics, and the price of our daily four-course lunch menu at Bar Roca was 450 pesetas, around U.S. $3.

The menu changed daily, but the first course was usually a simple green salad with a couple slices of tomato, olives, onion, and a hard-boiled egg. For the second course, the guest could choose between three or four light dishes—for example, green beans with serrano ham or escalivada, a roasted vegetable salad. The main course always offered a choice of protein. We served traditional dishes. Stewed rabbit was a favorite. So was the "lomo rebozado," slim slices of pork loin that would get an egg-and-flour wash before being pan-fried. The thin batter would puff when it cooked. I liked them best later on, after they had cooled. My cousin, Alex, and I would have contests to see who could eat the most slices.

Every Thursday we served paella, and people lined up for it in front of our tiny façade. Most of the people in the line worked in neighborhood factories. We were just five blocks away from the church of the Sagrada Família. Gaudí's most famous building is now Barcelona's most popular tourist destination, but back then there were no tourists, and the neighborhood still had a lot of industry. I can remember the Estrella Damm bottling plant. Every time I passed, I took a deep breath because I loved the strong smell of barley and yeast. I would always take a break to perch on the stairs by the front gate. From there I could catch a glimpse, through the large windows, of the giant machines filling the beer bottles inside. It was fascinating. Whenever I saw Estrella workers in the restaurant, I would wonder to myself if they got to operate those machines. What a cool job.

My own tasks at the time were not quite so interesting: sweeping and washing dishes. But I wanted to learn to cook. I was famous (still am) for asking dozens of questions, and I would bombard my grandmother with them while watching her. "Why do you cut these this way?" "How do you know when to take it out of the oven?" Eventually, I guess, she recognized an interest and started to teach me a few basics.

As I got older, I graduated to pulling espresso for regulars before heading to school, then returning after class to make bread pudding and help close up shop. My father saw a spark of interest, and when it came time to choose a career path, he offered to pay for culinary school. I liked the idea, but when I proposed it to my mom's side of the family, my grandmother instantly objected. "Don't do it," she advised. "You're crazy. Too much work. Too many long hours. Don't you see what we go through in this business?"

Despite her advice, I enrolled. I was the youngest in my class at Escola de Restauració i Hostalatge de Barcelona. Whenever I wasn't in class, I was working in restaurant kitchens—peeling potatoes, dicing onions, and picking up speed and discipline along the way.

In the years just after leaving school, I expanded my knowledge of Spanish cuisine. I had a job in the Catalonian Pyrenees and spent a summer cooking in the Canary Islands. At Gaig, a Michelin-starred Barcelona restaurant, I worked as a prep cook and saw many of the dishes I had originally learned to prepare with my family reinvented and reimagined. Seeing that food treated with such reverence and respect gave me an incredible sense of pride.

Later I worked stints in Barcelona and Paris, broadening my culinary knowledge along the way. At Alain Passard's L'Arpège, in Paris, I trained in the pastry station, where I learned to make their amazing mille-feuilles, the best version of this airy, custard-layered puff pastry I have ever eaten. Across the Seine at Restaurant Alain Ducasse, I learned that obsessing over ingredients and mastering simplicity could produce magical results. I still remember a dish of poached langoustines nestled in a reduced cream sauce that had been slowly infused with the langoustine heads. A dollop of osetra caviar topped the succulent shellfish. The simple combination was spectacular. I aspired to cook like that.

Once while I was working in Barcelona as a pastry chef, my friend Angel called me with exciting news. El Bulli, Ferran Adrià's famed restaurant on the Costa Brava, needed people to work the rest of the season. I jumped at the opportunity. But on my first day in the kitchen, I twisted my ankle. A doctor told me to stay off my feet for two weeks, but I couldn't throw away the chance to work with Adrià, so I taped up my ankle and kept going with the rest of the crew. The days were long and trying—in at 9:00 a.m. and out at midnight, with just one 15-minute break—but it was one of the best life and cooking experiences I ever had. It blew my mind to see how limitless culinary creativity could be.

My career continued to progress, and larger opportunities presented themselves. An offer to head the kitchen of a new Spanish restaurant in Miami pulled me away from my first executive chef position in Barcelona. The prospect of building a menu of Catalan classics for a fresh audience excited me. For inspiration I looked all the way back to the little kitchen at Bar Roca and to my family's

recipes, then transformed them with the technique and eye I had developed over my career. The food I made for that venture garnered attention, and landed me an offer to open the W Hotel restaurant in nearby South Beach.

It was during a trip with the W team to New York City that I first visited Boqueria. I had never eaten there before and didn't know anything about it when I walked into the SoHo restaurant that evening. The atmosphere struck me immediately. The place was packed, and I was captivated. I loved the music and lighting and enjoyed watching the chefs hard at work in the open kitchen from my seat at the large communal table in the center of the restaurant. I had often thought that the States had yet to capture the real energy of Spain in a restaurant, but that night in Boqueria, I thought, "This is amazing. They did it. It's perfect."

While we were eating, Yann stopped by our table to say hello. I talked to him for five or ten minutes, and in that short time, we were laughing. I had a good feeling about this place.

Back in Miami a few months later, a recruiter called me. "There's a company in New York. They have two Spanish restaurants and they're looking for an executive chef." I interrupted her: "Boqueria, right?" She fell silent for a second before asking, "How did you know?" I don't know how I knew. I just did. I hadn't stopped thinking about my experience at Boqueria, and about how I much I wanted to serve my food in that environment. It felt right. Just months later, I was rolling up the sleeves of my Boqueria chef coat for the first time.

I often think back to my grandmother's warning, that the life of a chef would be hard work. She was absolutely right. But, in this case, I'm glad I ignored her advice.

Quimet & Quimet, Barcelona, Spain

Our Food

We take our name from Barcelona's Boqueria Market. The sprawling expanse of masterfully merchandised stalls selling every food product imaginable sits just off La Rambla, the wide pedestrian artery of Barcelona's old city center. It has been in that same spot for hundreds of years, and in that time it has evolved into one of the world's greatest markets, an inspiring place for anyone who loves food. The world's most prized ingredients, such as Jamón Ibérico, sit alongside the freshest local seafood and vegetables. Pungent spice aromas mingle with the zesty scent of freshly squeezed citrus and the fragrance of just-pulled espresso.

Kioskos, or small tapas bars, sit along the perimeter of the market. Every morning their chefs walk the corridors to select the day's best produce, fish, and meat. These products drive the daily menu, which will be scrawled on a chalkboard or shouted to patrons over the din of the neighboring market. The menus weave together a mix of familiar dishes like croquetas and salt-cod fritters with specials featuring rare or prized ingredients, such as gooseneck barnacles from Galicia or sweet, incandescent orange shrimp from Palamòs on the Costa Brava.

At Boqueria, we create our menu in the same spirit. Every Friday Marc meets with the chefs from each of our restaurants to toss around ideas and experiment with new dishes. They have already visited the Union Square Greenmarket. Although it is much smaller than the Boqueria Market, it is charged with the same vitality and stocked with beautiful produce. Now the team gathers in the kitchen of our SoHo location with shopping bags overflowing with fresh ingredients. Some of those ingredients will become the stars of our "market menu" of seasonal specials; others will provide an important flourish or a finishing touch.

Marc starts with a list of ideas he'd like to try out, and the team gets to work. They take a first pass at each new dish. Marc is relentless as he pushes the staff for honest feedback. He makes laps around the restaurant with a new salad or tapa in hand, asking everyone working to taste. He presses for an honest opinion: "Qué?" He asks and watches intently as a manager takes a bite. His eyes widen while he looks for a reaction. "You like it? More lemon juice? Does it need something crunchy?"

Each dish is made several times over until everyone agrees that it's the best it can be. Even then, many dishes will never make it onto the market menu. Even fewer will shoulder their way onto the classic tapas menu between the paella and the pimientos. The (metaphorical) tapas bar is high.

On the Boqueria table, every dish must stand alone and stand out, each one fully composed and incorporating a variety of tastes and textures. Classic dishes such as patatas bravas and gambas al ajillo get fine-tuned to a New York buzz with an uptick in spice or an added texture. Other dishes celebrate traditional Spanish products in completely new ways; for example, a staple huevo estrellado (fried egg) sits under just-sliced Jamón Ibérico over homemade potato chips with a decadent truffled potato cream.

Often we look no further than the farmers' market for inspiration and celebrate the fresh, seasonal ingredients available to us here in New York City. Even in these dishes Marc always looks to incorporate a nod to Spain. A salad of fresh pears and radicchio finds balance with a shower of salty aged Mahón cheese. Crisp cauliflower comes to life when paired with a fragrant saffron dressing.

For the final test of each dish, we look back to the tapas bars of Spain. Their food is always easy to share and easier to love. That's what tapas are all about—dishes that inspire connection and conversation. We look for the connection at every service.

When a guest flags down a server to ask, "What's in that incredible sauce?"

When someone leans over the kitchen counter to take pictures of the sizzling seafood-packed plancha. "Are those the squid? I had them. They were amazing!"

When plates move around the table as quickly as the conversation.

That's the true measure of our success.

Waiting for Bruni

In 2006, when Boqueria opened, there was no Yelp, no Instagram, no Facebook, no competition for the old-guard media. The opinions of key restaurant critics could make or break a new restaurant. Shortly after its opening, in 2000, Yann's first restaurant, Suba, had received a harsh one-star review in the *New York Times*. It nearly killed the business, which took years to recover.

We weren't sure Boqueria would get reviewed (not every restaurant does), but we knew a *Times* review could make all the difference. We needed Frank Bruni, the *New York Times* food critic, to visit. And that review had to be good.

In those early months, we were always on the lookout for Bruni. Eventually, we spotted him. He came! And then he returned. We examined every detail of his visits for clues. Did he clean his plates? What facial expressions did he make? What tip did he leave? In the end, we could decipher nothing. We had no idea what he thought.

It was October when the *Times* contacted our publicist to let him know that a review was imminent. The paper sent a photographer in to take pictures of the dining room and a few select dishes, and Bruni called to interview Yann and our opening chef. Each step moved us closer toward the review, anxiety rising day by day.

In 2006 Spanish chefs were the darlings of the food world. Ferran Adrià's restaurant, El Bulli, on Catalonia's Costa Brava, had become a destination for culinary pilgrims. Basque chefs such as Martín Berasategui and Andoni Luis Aduriz had transformed San Sebastián into the city with the most Michelin stars per capita in the world. Spain was on the culinary map, but it had been put there by chef-driven fine dining restaurants, not by upscale tapas bars or "gastropubs."

We wanted to showcase the other Spanish cuisine, the delicious ingredient-driven dishes and Spanish classics that made the food at our favorite tapas bars so irresistible. The farm-to-table movement quickly gaining popularity in New York at the time seemed right in line with what tapas bars had been doing forever: talking to farmers, fishmongers, and foragers; cultivating relationships with the best meat and dairy purveyors; buying the best product possible every day and preparing it with care.

We hoped we had done that. Would Bruni feel the same? We had seen our dining room fill nightly with happy guests and had been reassured by their enthusiasm for the food, service, and space. Regulars started to return once or twice a week and bring in their friends. But it was still slow early in the week, especially outside prime dinner hours. A positive review in the *New York Times* would be the ultimate validation and would bring us the business we needed for real success.

What if Bruni didn't like it? What if we tried too hard to loosen up service? Did we make it so informal and friendly that it came over as too casual? Was he comfortable in the high bar-stool seating? *Did he like the food?*

Eventually, the *New York Times* gave us a heads-up. The review would be featured in the November 1, 2006 edition, and we knew that the reviews always post to the website first, appearing late on the night before the print editions hit newsstands.

Once service ended on Halloween night, Yann gathered the general manager and the opening chef at a back corner table. The review was due to post. They were spooked and huddled around a laptop, reloading the food section every minute or so. They took turns speculating, and with each passing minute the tension and their blood pressure rose.

Refresh. Still last week's review. Refresh. Still last week's review. Refresh. Refresh. Refresh. Still last week's review. Refresh, and then ... a headline: "Tapas: It's Not About Commitment." And just underneath? Two *New York Times* stars! Restaurants four times as ambitious had been given no stars at all. "Two stars! Two stars! We did it!"

The staff dropped their closing side work to hug and cheer and break out some cava for a toast while the others continued to read. The text spun on the page as they moved through the column hardly taking a single breath.

He liked the food! He liked the high seats! He thought the squid was "fantastic" and the lamb was "beautifully braised!" He said the cojonudo was "My kind of finger food." One sentence captured it best: "In New York it's easier to make like you're having tapas than to actually have them. The happy, peppy new Spanish restaurant Boqueria, named for the food market in Barcelona, is doing what it can to change that."

He got it! Years of dreaming and hard work had gone into building Boqueria, and Bruni had just given our future a green light. We were ecstatic.

La Xampanyeria, Barcelona, Spain

THE CLASSICS

THE CLASSICS

Recognizable to anyone who has spent time in Spain, these dishes, whose names are shouted nightly to bartenders over animated chatter in Spanish, Catalan, Gallego, and Basque, transport us across the Atlantic to our favorite tapas spots in just a couple of bites.

At Boqueria, we adapt these classics with a New York sensibility. It takes bravery to mess with patatas bravas,

but we like ours spicier. Every added twist should make a dish even harder to resist. Crisp mushroom croquettes get a dollop of pungent truffle allioli. A pop of pickled shallots and a dusting of black olive salt electrifies traditional grilled lamb skewers.

These are tapas in 3D—each dish invigorated by layers of texture, flavor, and temperature.

MONTADOS
Olive Oil Toasts

Serves
as many as you like

Every night, the cobblestoned streets of the Basque culinary capital, San Sebastián, fill with hungry people on a slow crawl from tapas bar to tapas bar. The counters in those bars are piled high with montados, small toasts topped with every imaginable ingredient. Built to tempt patrons into having just one more drink, these colorful toasts are easy to make and essential to your tapas spread.

Montados are incredibly versatile and it's fun to come up with interesting combinations in your own kitchen. Even your grandma's potato salad can become a tapa when served on our bite-sized olive oil toasts and dusted with some smoky pimentón. You don't need a lot to compile a provocative pairing. Just get a balance of salty, creamy, and bright.

All our montados start with toasts. They're incredibly easy to make and can be prepared up to a few hours ahead of time. As long as you start with good bread (it can even be day-old), you'll end up with good toasts.

Olive Oil Toasts

1 or more baguettes
extra-virgin olive oil
kosher salt

Preheat the oven to 450°F.

Cut a baguette into ½-inch slices and place in a single layer on a baking sheet. Sprinkle lightly with salt and drizzle with the oil.

Bake until golden brown and crisp around the edges but still soft in the centers, about 3 minutes. Don't overbake them or they'll end up tough.

You can use the toasts immediately or cool them to warm or room temperature.

MONTADOS DE ATÚN

Toasts with Tuna, Piquillos, and Caper Allioli

Makes
6

Prep
20 minutes

Total
20 minutes

6 Olive Oil Toasts (see page 32)
3 jarred piquillo peppers, patted dry
and seeded
6 ounces (approx.) bonito tuna,
preferably Ventresca, flaked into
large chunks
3 teaspoons Caper Allioli (recipe
follows)
coarsely chopped flat-leaf parsley
leaves, for garnish

Caper Allioli

Makes about ¾ cup
Prep 10 minutes
Cook 10 minutes

1 tablespoon drained capers, finely
chopped
¾ cup Spiced Allioli Dressing (see
page 273)

For these montados, a creamy, caper allioli ties together sweet peppers and
savory fish. Just be sure to buy the best tuna and piquillos you can find. (Order
them online!) La Catedral de Navarra makes the juiciest, sweetest, most delicate
piquillos, and there are a number of companies that jar delicious tuna, but we
love the Don Bocarte bonito del norte ventresca. Whichever brand you buy, just
be sure the fish comes in fillets packed in olive oil.

On each toast place half a piquillo pepper. Divide the tuna among the toasts
and then top with the allioli. Garnish with parsley. Serve immediately.

Stir the capers and allioli dressing together in a small bowl. Stir in 1–2
tablespoons water to loosen the mixture.

Montados de Atún (page 33)

Bonito del Norte

In the Basque country and Cantabria, fishermen brave the often cold, rough waters of the Bay of Biscay to fish for bonito del norte, a fatty albacore tuna native to the area. Most of the catch ends up being conserved in jars and cans. Unlike in the States, where sub-prime tuna is destined for canning, in Spain the choicest fish is set aside for preserving. It is a time-honored tradition. Fishermen bring the daily catch into seaside factories that process the fish and preserve it in top-quality Spanish olive oil.

But this is not industrialized food. In these plants, every fish is butchered and cleaned by hand. Small armies of women in clean smocks and hairnets fuss over the filets with tweezers and scissors to make sure they are perfect. Others carefully place the fish into cans and jars before sending these off to be filled with the oil. The painstaking care in selection and processing is evident in every bite. The succulent fish is celebrated all over Spain, where it is used in all variety of salads and tapas.

The pale white flesh of bonito del norte is more tender and silkier than the skipjack in standard American cans. This is one case in which domestic varieties just can't substitute. Look for imported jars or cans with whole bonito fillets packed in olive oil. The best of the best is ventresca, the rich and fatty belly of the tuna.

Anchovies

Anchovies vary widely in quality. Get the best. (Cheap ones tend to taste overly fishy and way too salty.) Even if you already love these fish, you'll love them even more if you splurge a little. Our favorites come from Cantabria, a region along Spain's northern coast. It fronts the Bay of Biscay, a gulf of strong currents and waves that make the silvery fish especially fatty.

Once caught, the fish are filleted by hand. Those destined for canning are aged and salt-cured, then lightly rinsed and packed in olive oil. The savory fish ends up meaty and succulent. Those chosen for boquerones (white anchovies) are lightly pickled and marinated in a vinegar-olive oil blend, which gives them a flavor that is a perfect balance of tangy and rich. You can order good anchovies online and buy boquerones from the refrigerated section of a Spanish specialty store or a well-stocked market.

The highest-quality versions of both kinds of anchovy are delicious enough to eat on their own. They're also great on montados, wrapped around olives, or draped on Pan con Tomate (see page 47).

MONTADOS DE ANCHOAS

Salt-Cured Anchovies and Eggplant on Toast

Makes
6

Prep
20 minutes

Total
30 minutes

1 Japanese eggplant, or small
   ordinary eggplant
1 teaspoon extra-virgin olive oil
1 teaspoon sherry vinegar
6 Olive Oil Toasts (see page 32)
6 teaspoons labneh
12 salt-cured anchovies
12 basil leaves
kosher salt and freshly ground
   black pepper

In northern Spain, anchovies are often salt-cured and preserved in olive oil, resulting in mild and meaty fillets. Look for our favorite Don Bocarte anchovies from Cantabria to use in this recipe. In this pairing, the smoky creaminess of eggplant blackened over fire is the perfect counterpoint to the savory anchovies. Tangy labneh consummates that marriage beautifully in this summery two-bite montado. Since you've got the grill going anyway, toast the bread on the grate for an extra bit of smokiness.

Heat a charcoal grill to high. Alternatively you can use a burner on a gas range, turned to high, with a rack placed over it.

Set the eggplant on the grate over the hot flame. Cook, turning occasionally, until the skin is really black all around and the flesh is bubbling and collapsed, about 8–12 minutes. Transfer to a cutting board.

When the eggplant is cool enough to handle, discard the top, then peel off the skin. Cut the flesh in half crosswise, then cut each half into thirds lengthwise. Transfer to a bowl, season with salt and pepper, and drizzle with the oil and vinegar. Gently mix, keeping the pieces intact.

For each montado, spread 1 teaspoon labneh on the toast, then arrange 1 eggplant piece and 2 anchovies on top. Top with a couple of basil leaves and serve immediately.

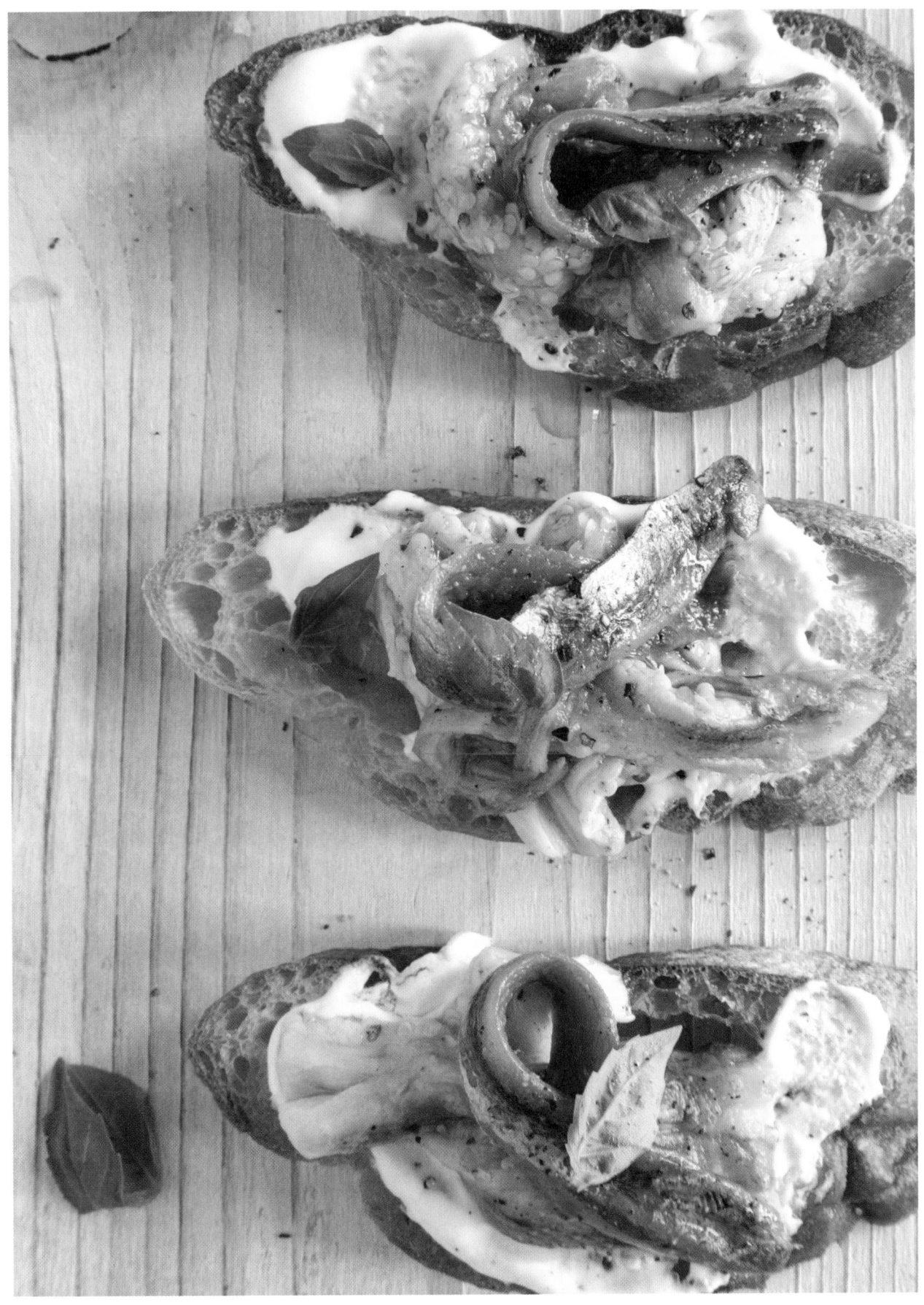

MONTADOS DE BOQUERONES

Marinated Anchovies and Olive Relish on Toast

Makes
1 dozen

Prep
20 minutes

Total
20 minutes

Boquerones, mild white anchovies marinated in white wine vinegar and olive oil, are so succulent and they're delicious alone on toasts. We've highlighted their tangy richness by setting them over creamy cheese, alongside sweet roasted tomatoes and a savory green olive relish. Each bite is a riot of textures and big flavors that is improved only by a glass of vermouth or sangría (see pages 252–261).

12 Olive Oil Toasts (see page 32)
4 ounces goat cheese, softened
12 sundried tomato halves in olive oil, preferably Divina brand, drained
12 boquerones
Olivada Relish (recipe follows)
snipped chives, for serving

For each toast: spread 2 teaspoons goat cheese on the toast, then top with 1 tomato piece, 1 boquerón, and 1 teaspoon olivada relish. Serve immediately.

Olivada Relish

Makes about ½ cup
Prep 10 minutes
Total 10 minutes

8 large green Spanish olives, such as Gordal or Manzanilla
8 sundried tomato halves in olive oil, drained and very finely chopped, preferably Divina brand
1 tablespoon finely chopped capers
1 tablespoon finely chopped cornichons
¼ teaspoon finely chopped rosemary
¼ teaspoon finely chopped guindilla pepper, or crushed red chili flakes

Pit the olives by cutting off the flesh alongside the stones. Chop the flesh very finely and mix with the remaining ingredients in a small bowl.

COJONUDO

Chorizo and Fried Quail Eggs on Toasts

Makes
1 dozen

Prep
2 minutes

Total
12 minutes

1 (5-inch) link cured spicy chorizo
12 Olive Oil Toasts (see page 32)
extra-virgin olive oil
12 quail eggs
Maldon sea salt flakes

Legend has it that the king of Spain once ate this stack of chorizo and fried egg on toast and declared it "cojonudo" (that's slang for "fucking good"). Whether or not that story of this iconic montado from Castile y León is true, it's undeniable that the dish is "cojonudo."

Spicy chorizo juices and runny egg yolk soak into toast when your teeth sink into this canapé; it's the perfect bite and we're not messing with it.

Remove and discard the chorizo's paper casing. Cut diagonally into twelve ¼-inch-thick slices. (Reserve the ends for another use.)

Heat a large skillet over high heat until hot. Add the chorizo slices in a single layer and cook just until shiny as the fat starts to render, about 3 seconds per side. Immediately transfer each slice to a piece of toast.

Heat ½ teaspoon olive oil in a nonstick pan over medium heat. Crack as many eggs as will fit in a single layer without overlapping; work in batches if necessary. Cook until the whites are set and the yolk is runny, about 2 minutes. Immediately place on top of the chorizo on the toasts. Repeat this step with any remaining eggs, using ½ teaspoon oil per batch.

Sprinkle the eggs with the salt flakes and serve immediately.

Chorizo

In shops and market stalls throughout Spain, "carniceros" (butchers) hawk a wide variety of fresh and cured pork sausages. Dozens of cured chorizos, the most popular variety, hang from the rafters of every butcher shop. The bright red pork sausage gets its color and much of its flavor from pimentón (see below). The texture is similar to a cured salami, but the flavor is much smokier. The most delicious varieties are made from the same acorn-fed Ibérico pigs as Spain's premium Ibérico ham. Here, in the States, cured chorizo is easily ordered online or found in well-stocked markets. Peel off any paper casing before slicing the links to serve as part of a cured meat platter or to brown lightly and add to a dish.

Pimentón

Pimentón is Spain's most utilized spice. The bright red paprika lends its flavor to innumerable typical dishes. In Galicia it is dusted on octopus. In Rioja, it clings to the region's famous Patatas a la Riojana. All over Spain, it flavors stews and dusts montados. Chorizo, sobrasada, and all the other vibrant red sausages of Spain, fresh or cured, get their stunning color and deep flavor from it.

The spice, produced principally in Spain's hot and dusty south and west comes in a variety flavors. The distinguished growing regions of La Vera in Extremadura and Murcia in Spain's warm south produce the best. Producers use different peppers to create powders of varying spice and sweetness, but it is the smoking process that gives the spice a rich meaty flavor that adds savory depth to its sweet and tangy aroma.

As you can probably tell by the recipes in this book, we go through a lot of pimentón at Boqueria. Our pantry is always stocked with several varieties. At home you will find it to be a perfect addition to marinades and vinaigrettes. It's especially great for vegetarian dishes. When sprinkled on eggs or potatoes its rich smokiness mimics the satisfying flavor of bacon or chorizo.

BOQUERIA

PAN CON TOMATE

Country Bread Rubbed with Garlic, Tomato, and Olive Oil

Serves
as many as you like

This is the most important recipe in this book. Why? Because it takes five of the most ordinary ingredients in your kitchen (bread, olive oil, tomato, garlic, and salt) and with little need for cooking or technique transforms them into something extraordinary.

"Pa amb Tomàquet," as it is called in Catalonia, is the national dish. To make it, fresh garlic and tomato are rubbed against toasted bread. The rough craggy craters grate and capture the ingredients. A good olive oil is drizzled over and a sprinkle of salt finishes it off. The preparation takes seconds but the result is timeless, a combination so perfect it has accompanied every meal in Catalonia for centuries.

You most likely have the ingredients for this in your pantry all the time, so you should make it all the time! In the restaurants we serve it on its own or accompanied by cured meats and cheeses. We use it to make rustic sandwiches with Jamón Serrano and Manchego cheese, and a plate of pan con tomate served with mixed greens and an extra thick slice of Tortilla Española (see page 96) is one of our most popular lunch and brunch dishes. We think this should be on every table in the restaurant.

While you can make do with almost any garlic, bread, salt, olive oil, and tomatoes, choosing some of these ingredients specifically for this dish will give you the best results. The bread should be crusty on the outside with big yeasty bubbles on the inside. Choose a good first-press, extra virgin Spanish olive oil and a salt with texture—flaky Maldon is our favorite. The garlic should be firm and fresh and the tomatoes should be fleshy and ripe.

---

crusty country bread sliced
½-inch thick
kosher salt
extra-virgin olive oil
1 garlic clove
1 heirloom ripe tomato

Preheat the broiler and position a rack 6 inches below the heating element.

Lightly sprinkle both sides of the bread with salt and drizzle with the oil. Toast the bread on one side until browned, then flip and toast the other side just until crisp. Watch it carefully; broilers vary greatly in strength, and some burn bread fast.

Gently rub garlic over the toast. Cut a ripe tomato in half, seed it if it's watery, and rub the cut sides into the bread, getting the pulp well into any nooks of the toast. Drizzle with olive oil and sprinkle with salt. Cut into pieces if you like and serve immediately.

Clockwise from left: Rabo de Buey con Albaricoques (page 212); Espinacas a la Catalana (page 111); Patatas Bravas (page 57); Albóndigas con Gambas (page 196)

PINTXOS MORUNOS

Grilled Spiced Lamb Skewers

Makes
8 to 10 skewers

Prep
20 minutes

Total
45 minutes plus 2 days' marinating

All throughout Andalucía, you can practically smell these skewers in the air. They're the region's most popular and iconic dish, mingling the primal seductive scent of grilled fatty lamb with heady spices toasted by fire. That combo comes from the Moors, who ruled much of the country for centuries. Their generous use of the warm spices commonly found in North African dishes brings a whole different dimension to Spanish cuisine. Here, fragrant cumin and coriander mingle with the bite of black pepper and the anise edge of fennel seeds, making the meat intensely spiced but not at all "spicy" in the fire-breathing chili sense.

All those spices, along with a topping of pickled shallots and lemony salsa verde, make each bite of marinated meat insanely flavorful. The bright salsa runs through the rich meaty juices like an avalanche, landing in crackling slices of country bread. Best. Toast. Ever.

---

2 teaspoons cumin seeds

2 teaspoons coriander seeds

2 teaspoons black peppercorns

2 teaspoons fennel seeds

¼ large sweet white Spanish onion, very thinly sliced

3 tablespoons hot pimentón (smoked paprika)

⅓ cup fresh lemon juice

4 cups blended canola-olive oil

1 pound 14 ounces boneless lamb top round (from the leg of lamb; you may need to source from a butcher), extra fat and gristle discarded, meat cut into 1-inch cubes

1 cup Pickling Liquid (see page 270)

2 shallots, sliced ¹⁄₁₆-inch-thick crosswise, rings separated

country bread, for serving

Salsa Verde (see page 275), for serving

kosher salt

You will need:
8–10 (7-inch) bamboo skewers

Combine the cumin, coriander, peppercorns, and fennel in a small skillet. Toast over medium-high heat, stirring often, until golden and fragrant, 2–3 minutes. Cool completely, then grind well in a spice grinder. (Or use a mortar and pestle.)

Transfer the ground spices to a large bowl and add the onion, pimentón, lemon juice, and 1 tablespoon salt. Stir well, then stir in the oil.

Thread 5 lamb cubes onto each skewer, pressing them together tightly. Pack the skewers into an airtight container that will fit the skewers snugly, then pour the marinade over the meat. Seal the container and marinate for at least 2 days or up to 5 days.

Bring the pickling liquid to a boil. Pack the shallots into a jar or other airtight container. Pour the boiling liquid over the shallots and seal the jar. Let sit until room temperature, at least 1 hour. The pickled shallots can be refrigerated for up to 1 month.

When ready to serve, remove the skewered lamb from the marinade and season with salt. Heat a large skillet over high heat until very hot. Add enough skewers to fit in a single layer without crowding. Cook until the bottom is well browned, about 2 minutes, then turn and sear the opposite side. Cook for about 1 more minute for medium-rare. Repeat with the remaining skewers.

Serve immediately on toasted country bread, topped with the salsa verde and pickled shallots.

DÁTILES CON BEICON

Bacon-Wrapped Dates

Makes
as many as you like

Prep
20 minutes

Total
45 minutes

Four ingredients—one outstanding appetizer. These simple crowd-pleasers are so good that we haven't messed with them since we dished them out at our first friends and family pre-opening meal. Every single diner raved about these that first night. Ten years on, they still love them. Sweet dates and salty bacon are delicious enough on their own, but we stuff the dates with pungent Valdeón blue cheese and tender Marcona almonds for a knock-out punch of flavor.

You can make as many or as few of these as you'd like. Our Upper East Side prep cook, Rosa, made 25,383 of them last year! They're a great party dish as they're so quick to prepare. You can make them ahead of time and just pop them in the oven when you're ready to serve.

We enjoy a good date. We politely pass on the drier standard versions and opt for the bigger, sweeter varieties. Medjools are best, but Deglet Noors work too.

Medjool dates
Marcona almonds, roasted and salted
Valdeón cheese, or other mild creamy
   blue cheese, such as Gorgonzola
applewood-smoked bacon (½ slice per
   date)

You will need:
small skewers. We use 1 for every 3
   dates, but you can skewer the dates
   individually or in pairs if you prefer.
   Soak the skewers in water for at least
   30 minutes.

Preheat the oven to 400°F. Line a half sheet pan with foil.

Cut a slit lengthwise in a date and pull out the pit. Put 1 almond inside the date, then spread ½ teaspoon cheese in the cavity. Close the date around the stuffing, completely sealing the edges as tightly as possible by pressing the cut edges of the date together. Wrap half a slice of bacon tightly around the date; the slice should overlap itself by at least one full rotation. Repeat to make as many as you'd like.

Place three bacon-wrapped dates side by side, close together. Insert a skewer through them. Repeat with the remaining bacon-wrapped dates.

Place the skewers on the prepared pan, spacing them an inch apart. Bake, turning once, until the bacon is evenly browned and its fat is rendered, about 12 minutes each side.

SALTEADO DE SETAS

Sautéed Wild Mushrooms with Aged Manchego Cheese

Serves
4 to 6

Prep
30 minutes

Total
45 minutes

1 pound 2 ounces wild mushrooms, preferably a mix of creminis, shiitakes, yellow oysters, trumpet royales, and oysters

6 tablespoons extra-virgin olive oil

3 garlic cloves, very thinly sliced

2 sprigs of thyme

1 lemon

1 teaspoon sherry vinegar

2 ounces aged Manchego cheese, for serving

½ teaspoon finely chopped flat-leaf parsley

kosher salt

freshly ground black pepper

In the Pyrenees of Catalonia and the Basque Country, cooks make a sport of foraging for a range of wild mountain mushroom varieties. Here in New York we use whatever we find at the market—meaty creminis, silky shiitakes, or frilly oysters—in this quick mushroom sauté with caramelized garlic and olive oil. To add another dimension, we top the dish with shredded Manchego cheese and a salad of matchstick-sliced trumpet royale mushrooms in lemon and parsley.

Cut 1 trumpet royale mushroom into thin matchsticks; reserve in a small bowl. (Alternatively, you can use a cremini or other mushroom suitable for eating raw.) Cut the remaining mushroom caps and flat pieces into ½-inch pieces. Break any cluster mushrooms into ½-inch chunks.

Combine the oil and garlic in a large skillet. Set over high heat and cook, stirring, until the garlic becomes golden brown around the edges, about 1 minute. Add the mushrooms and thyme and generously season with salt. Cook, stirring, until the mushrooms are evenly coated with the oil and salt, then spread the pieces in an even layer. Let them sit for a few minutes to brown the bottoms, then stir occasionally until the mushrooms are shiny and just starting to stick to the pan, about 6 minutes total.

Remove from the heat and remove the thyme sprigs. Zest and juice the lemon and set the zest aside. Stir in 1 teaspoon of the juice along with the vinegar; season to taste with more salt if necessary. Transfer to a serving plate. Sprinkle the lemon zest on top of the mixture, then slice enough Manchego on top to cover.

Drizzle 1 teaspoon each of oil and lemon juice over the reserved raw mushrooms. Season with salt, then toss in the parsley. Mound on top of the cooked mushroom mixture and serve immediately.

BOQUERIA

PATATAS BRAVAS

Fried Potatoes with Spicy Tomato Sauce and Allioli

Serves
4 to 8

Prep
30 minutes

Total
1 hour

Like many of our sister tapas bars across the Atlantic, we aspire to create unique dishes that guests will remember and make them return. And just like them we find that no matter what we add to the menu, no dish will ever have the draw of this simplest classic. When we realized that Patatas Bravas would always be our top seller, we knew they would also have to be the best.

"Patatas Bravas" translates literally to "brave potatoes," a name that hints to the spiciness of the dish. Spaniards, however, typically shy away from fiery foods, and what counts as heat in more traditional versions of this dish doesn't even register for most Americans. In our recipe we take the spice up a few notches by adding fiery dried guindilla peppers to the smooth tomato sauce. We dust the cooked potatoes in two different kinds of Spanish paprika and smother them in the rich sauce and a cool, garlicky allioli. The golden-fried potato wedges are crisp on first bite and airy and light inside.

---

5 large Yukon Gold potatoes
   (2½ pounds)
extra-virgin olive oil for frying
   (see instructions)
½ teaspoon hot pimentón
½ teaspoon sweet pimentón
1 portion Salsa Brava (see page 275)
1 portion Allioli (see page 273)
kosher salt

Peel the potatoes, then cut them into quarters. Cut each quarter lengthwise into ½-inch wedges.

Put the potatoes in a large bowl and cover with cold water. Swish the pieces to lose all their starch; this will prevent the pieces from sticking to one another while frying. Lift the pieces out of the water and into a colander. Repeat this step until the water is clear after swishing. Transfer the potatoes to paper towels and press until very, very dry.

Pour the oil into a large Dutch oven. The amount of oil required will depend on the size of the Dutch oven; it should be enough to cover the potatoes by a couple of inches. Heat the oil over medium-high heat. To test that it is hot enough for frying, drop in a potato wedge; it should sizzle immediately. If not, continue heating the oil.

Very carefully add all of the potatoes. (Depending on the size of your Dutch oven you may need to do this in batches.) The oil should immediately bubble and boil vigorously. Raise the heat to high. Fry, stirring every once in a while to cook evenly. Don't stir too much or you'll risk breaking the pieces. The goal is to get the potatoes crisp and dark brown on the outside and soft inside. It will take about 30 minutes total.

Set a colander over a bowl. Use a slotted spoon to transfer the potatoes to the colander to drain a bit, then transfer to a large, wide bowl. Generously season with salt and both pimentones. Gently toss until the potatoes are evenly seasoned.

Transfer to serving dishes and serve immediately with the salsa brava and allioli on the side for dipping and drizzling all over.

Chef's tip: Be sure to use a very large and wide Dutch oven so the oil doesn't bubble over. It should have at least a 5-quart capacity. A heavy saucepot would work, too.

Guindilla

"Guindilla" is the Castillian Spanish word for any of a variety of spicy chili peppers. In Spain, many of the small spicy chilies used to add heat to dishes are imported from Asia and South America. At Boqueria we use a small dried variety called "ojo de pájaro," or bird's-eye, chilis. They are no bigger than a sunflower seed but pack more punch than a jalapeño.

If you can't find dried bird's-eye chilies, dried Mexican chili peppers are the perfect substitute and are readily available in most American supermarkets. The smaller varieties, such as de árbol, tepin, and piquín, come closest in heat and flavor to a bird's-eye.

CROQUETAS DE JAMÓN IBÉRICO
Iberian Ham Croquettes

Makes
about 40

Prep
1 hour

Total
1½ hours plus cooling

Marc arrived at Boqueria eager to add new dishes to the menu, but his most important mission was to pick apart and perfect Boqueria guest favorites. He obsessed over the croquetas. He knew that a passable croqueta could still be easy to love, but that an expertly executed croqueta is an irresistible glimpse into another dimension. Heaven, breaded and fried.

The barometer of a Spanish restaurant, croquetas may not be the flashiest item on the menu, but they'll tell you how good the kitchen is. From the breading to the béchamel, everything has to be just right. Marc knew he had to take them up a notch, and almost two years of trial and error, tweaks and adjustments resulted in the recipe we use today.

Perfection perfected comes from great ingredients. In this case, that means that the better the jámon, the better the croquetas. Ibérico de bellota is the best you can get, but if you can't find that, go for Serrano. Die-hard Ibérophiles might have a whole leg of Ibérico hanging around. If you are so lucky, you can use the off-cuts and trimmings to dice for the filling and you can simmer the bone in the milk for more porky goodness. Otherwise, buy thick slices to cut.

To balance the savory jámon, we serve the croquetas with a sweet and tangy quince salsa for dipping.

¼ pound plus 1 tablespoon (9 tablespoons in total) unsalted butter, cut into cubes

½ large white Spanish onion, very finely diced

2½ cups whole milk

2½ cups heavy cream

1 cup all-purpose flour

¾ pound Jamón Ibérico, cut into ¼-inch dice (2 cups)

kosher salt

6 cups fine store-bought breadcrumbs

6 large eggs

canola oil, for frying

Membrillo Salsa (recipe follows), for dipping

Place the butter and onion in a large saucepan. Cook over medium heat, stirring occasionally, until the onion is translucent and soft, but not browned, about 20 minutes. Meanwhile, combine the milk and cream in another saucepan and bring to a boil. Remove from heat.

Add the flour to the onion and stir well for 1 minute, then reduce the heat to medium-low. Continue stirring while pouring in 1 cup of the milk mixture in a steady stream; be sure to add this gradually to prevent lumps from forming. Continue adding the milk mixture 1 cup at a time, stirring well. Wait until the liquid is absorbed and the mixture is smooth before adding the next cupful; each addition should take about 5–7 minutes.

Add the jamón and stir well until it is evenly distributed. Remove from the heat. Season to taste with salt, then transfer to a large bowl. Press a piece of plastic wrap directly against the surface and refrigerate until the mixture is cold, at least 4 hours.

Form the mixture into cylinders measuring about 3 x 1 inches by scooping the mixture, then rolling with your hands. If the mixture has softened too much, refrigerate again. Put half of the breadcrumbs in a shallow dish. Beat one of the eggs in another shallow dish. Roll each cylinder in the crumbs to coat, shake off excess, then roll in the egg to coat. Finally, roll again in the crumbs to coat well. Use the remaining crumbs and egg when you run out or when the crumbs become too clumpy.

Fill a large saucepan with oil to a depth of 3 inches. Have ready a few wire racks covered with paper towels. Heat the oil over medium-high heat to 375ºF measured on a deep-fry thermometer. Add the cylinders to the hot oil, one at a time. Work in batches, adding only as many as will fit in the saucepan without crowding. Cook, carefully turning to brown evenly, until the croquettes are dark brown outside and hot inside, about 1 minute. Use a slotted spoon to transfer to the racks to drain. Repeat with the remaining croquettes.

Serve hot or warm with the membrillo salsa for dipping.

Chef's tip: If you have leftover egg from dipping the croquetas, flip it into a delicious omelet

Membrillo Salsa

Makes about 1¾ cups
Prep 5 minutes
Total 15 minutes

11 ounces membrillo (quince paste), diced (1¾ cups)
½ cup water
½ teaspoon sherry vinegar

Combine the membrillo and the water in a small saucepan. Cook over medium-high heat, stirring occasionally, until the membrillo dissolves and the mixture is smooth, about 7 minutes. Cool to room temperature, stirring occasionally.

The mixture should be thin enough for dipping. If not, stir in 1–2 tablespoons water. Stir in the vinegar and serve.

Croquetas de Jamón Ibérico (page 60)

Croquetas

Croquetas must be Spain's most irresistible tapa. The breaded and fried torpedo shapes sit on every tapas bar, tempting you to indulge in the gooey greatness of warm béchamel. Once you give in and take a bite, the crisp shell shatters into a thick, creamy filling studded with jamón, chicken, or mushrooms. The best ones keep the center in a blissful state of light creaminess.

These delicacies were created as a way to use up leftovers, but you will love them more than any main dish. The rich but neutral béchamel base accommodates almost any ingredient. Our recipe uses Ibérico ham, but you can always swap the ham for any cooked meat, seafood, or vegetable and use the same basic recipe with excellent results.

Back at our SoHo location in 2015, the then general manager, Cassidy, and the assistant GM, Franshelly, were both expecting babies at the same time. The physical demands of restaurant work are hard on anyone, but can be especially rough for somebody who is pregnant. But each of these dedicated women managed to work straight through until just a few weeks before they were due, taking care of Boqueria SoHo during its busy holiday season and leading us to a record-breaking year. While we credit that to their talent and fortitude, they credit occasional 20-minute office breaks with a plate of croquetas.

Although nutritionists may not put fried morsels of béchamel at the top of their super-foods list, our evidence suggests otherwise. We welcomed little Penelope and Lennox to the Boqueria family in early 2016, and their mothers were each promoted shortly thereafter.

PIMIENTOS DE PADRÓN

Blistered Green Peppers with Coarse Sea Salt

Serves
2 to 4

Prep
5 minutes

Total
10 minutes

"Be careful. About one in seven is really spicy." Our servers and food runners repeat this phrase whenever they place this dish on a table. For some guests, it's a warning. For others, a challenge. The little game of Spanish roulette is fun, and the combination of peppers, salt, and oil is effortlessly delicious.

The Spanish peppers from the Galician village of Padrón tend to be mild and almost fruity with fiery exceptions. If you can't find Padrones, Japanese shishito peppers taste very similar and are readily available here. Whichever variety we have on hand, we sizzle them in olive oil, then coat them with fine salt so they're evenly seasoned. For a hit of crunch, we finish the dish with a flurry of flaky salt.

---

extra-virgin olive oil
30 Padrón or shishito peppers
   (7 ounces)
fine sea salt
Maldon sea salt flakes

Line a large plate or wire rack with paper towels. Fill a large skillet with oil to a depth of ¼ inch. Heat over high heat until smoking. If you touch a pepper to the oil, it should sizzle immediately; if it doesn't, let the oil heat more.

Add all of the peppers in a single layer. Cook, continuously turning with tongs, until the skin blisters, becoming a paler green with dark charred spots, 2–5 minutes. Smaller peppers will be ready first, so remove them as they're done. Transfer to the paper towels to drain.

Gently shake the peppers in the towels to remove excess oil. Transfer to a serving plate and sprinkle with the fine and flaky salts.

BUÑUELOS DE BACALAO
Salt Cod and Potato Fritters

Makes
about 40

Prep
1 hour

Total
1½ hours plus desalting and cooling

Helping out in the family restaurants while growing up, Marc learned to prepare every menu staple in Spain. He could make bases like béchamel and allioli from scratch without a recipe and felt confident behind the stove, but his first internship in a fine-dining kitchen changed his view of those classic dishes forever.

At 18 years old he spent some time as an apprentice at Can Gaig, a storied Barcelona restaurant with a history that reaches back to the 1800s. This was his first experience in a Michelin starred restaurant and Marc watched the preparation of every dish with rapt attention. To his surprise, many of the dishes on the menu could have been lifted right from the daily lunch specials at Bar Roca, the little bar-restaurant his mother ran near the Sagrada Família. His family recipes were delicious, enviable even, but at Can Gaig, Marc saw these dishes elevated to a level he had never before imagined. He saw traditional canelones transformed when painstaking attention was paid to the architecture of a béchamel, the pasta made from scratch, and the freshest farm-raised chickens roasted and ground for the filling. He was inspired.

These buñuelos, which Marc learned to make while working there, exemplify the Can Gaig spirit of transforming everyday staples into something much more. In this recipe, creamy potatoes bind garlicky salt cod. At first bite, the little golden fritters release a burst of salty seaside air. The whipped potato is studded by islands of soft potato chunks and threaded with wisps of chewy bacalao. At Boqueria, we balance the briny goodness and steamy warmth with a cooling citrus mayonnaise.

1¼ pounds bacalao (salt cod, such as Cristobal Salted Cod Fillets)

1¼ pounds Idaho potatoes (about 5 medium), peeled and cut into 1½-inch chunks

5 tablespoons extra-virgin olive oil

3 small garlic cloves, very finely chopped

⅓ cup all-purpose flour

1 tablespoon, packed, finely chopped flat-leaf parsley

2 large eggs, at room temperature

olive oil, for frying

Citrus Mayonnaise (recipe follows)

Place the bacalao in a deep dish and cover with cold water. Cover the dish with plastic wrap and refrigerate for 36 hours, changing the water three times in the process. Drain well and cut a small piece to taste. It should taste like salted fish, but not excessively salty. If it does, cover with cold water and soak for another 6–12 hours, tasting after 6 hours to test for readiness. Drain well and cut into 1½-inch chunks. Remove and discard any bones.

Place the potatoes in a large saucepan and add enough cold water to cover by 2 inches. Bring to a boil over high heat, then boil until a cake tester or thin-bladed knife slides through easily, about 10 minutes. Avoid overcooking them; if they are soft they'll become watery. Drain well.

While the potatoes are boiling, place the bacalao in another saucepan and add enough cold water to cover by 1 inch. Bring to a boil over medium-high heat. When the water comes to a rolling boil, remove from the heat. Set a strainer over a large liquid measuring cup or a bowl and pour the bacalao into this. Reserve the drained bacalao and ⅔ cup of its cooking water. Discard the remaining cooking water.

Combine the oil and garlic in a large clean saucepan. Set over medium heat and cook, stirring occasionally, until the garlic is fragrant and just turning golden, about 4 minutes. Immediately add the flour and cook, stirring continuously, until the mixture is smooth and bubbling, about 1 minute. While stirring, pour in half of the bacalao water in a steady stream. Stir until smooth, then add the remaining water in the same manner. Stir in the parsley and remove from the heat.

Transfer the mixture to the bowl of a stand mixer fitted with the paddle attachment, along with the drained bacalao and potatoes. Beat on low speed until well mixed and slightly cooled, about 1 minute. Scrape the sides of the bowl. With the mixer on low speed, add the eggs one at a time, waiting for the first to be fully absorbed before adding the second and scraping the bowl occasionally. As soon as the eggs are fully incorporated, stop mixing. You want the mixture to include some chunks of potato and cod. Press a piece of plastic wrap directly against the surface of the mixture and refrigerate until cold, at least 3 hours. It will keep in an airtight container for up to 3 days.

Line a wire rack with paper towels. Fill a large saucepan with oil to a depth of 3 inches. Heat over medium-high heat until it registers 375°F on a deep-fry thermometer. Scoop up one heaped tablespoon of the bacalao mixture. Use another spoon to press and scrape the mixture against the first spoon to form an oval shape. Press and scrape the mixture once more, this time carefully dropping it into the hot oil. Repeat with more of the bacalao mixture until the buñuelos form a single layer in the saucepan without crowding. Fry, turning gently, until puffed and evenly golden brown, 1–2 minutes. Use a slotted spoon to transfer the buñuelos to the paper towels to drain. Let the oil heat up again and repeat with the remaining bacalao mixture, working in batches as necessary.

Serve the buñuelos hot or warm with the mayonnaise for dipping.

Citrus Mayonnaise

Makes 2¼ cups

1 orange
1 lemon
1 large egg
½ teaspoon white wine vinegar
¼ teaspoon Dijon mustard
½ teaspoon kosher salt
2 cups canola-olive blended oil

Remove the zest of half of the orange and place it in a blender. Squeeze 2 tablespoons orange juice and add to the zest. Remove the zest of half of the lemon, place it in the blender, and add 1 tablespoon lemon juice. Add the egg, vinegar, mustard, and salt. Blend on low until well mixed.

Gradually raise the speed to medium and add the oil in a slow, steady stream through the feed tube. As soon as the mixture is thickened and smooth, turn off the blender (over-blending can cause the mayonnaise to split).

Buñuelos de Bacalao (page 66)

Bacalao

Bacalao, known as salt cod in English, was the smartphone of medieval Europe—a leap in progress no one knew they wanted, but then couldn't live without. The salting technique, developed by medieval fisherman to dry and preserve cod caught on distant shores, turned a fragile, perishable product into a reliable staple with a long shelf life. It became an abundant and hot commodity throughout the Western world, driving the Spanish economy and fundamentally altering the course of history. Although born of necessity, this savory dried fish has become a much-loved delicacy.

When you stroll through the Parte Vieja of San Sebastián, you'll see bacalao planks hanging in shop windows. Step through the door and you'll be hit by the scent of sea air. Shopkeepers take orders from customers eager to get the perfect piece for a favorite family dish. They cut away at the stiff-as-board sheets and wrap each piece carefully in parchment. Once at home in the kitchen, a cook will drop the bacalao in water to begin the rehydration process. It may be a couple of days before this cod finds its way onto the dinner table, but the best things take time.

We may not have bacalao shops on our shores, but we can buy it online or in well-stocked markets. Just be sure to thoroughly soak and drain it repeatedly before using. It's important to get rid of what preserved it in the first place. When you do, you'll discover the most deeply flavorful cod—a fish that changed the world.

SALADS

SALADS

When Marc first arrived in New York, it was late summer and markets were at their peak, stocked with vine-ripened tomatoes, crisp cucumbers and summer squash, carrots every color of the rainbow, multiple varieties of every fresh herb on earth, and an endless selection of greens and lettuces. The bounty was inspiring. Even more inspiring was the appetite that New Yorkers had for these ingredients.

In Spain salads are often made up of just two or three ingredients, usually lettuce, tomato, and onion. They are sometimes studded with plump green olives and always dressed in oil and vinegar. But in New York, light eaters want bolder flavors. They expect salads with contrasting textures and surprising combinations of ingredients. This was new territory for Marc, and he relished the opportunity to get to know different ingredients and to create salads that satisfied this demand with a Spanish touch.

MELÓN CON JAMÓN

Melon with Iberian Ham and Fresh Herbs

Serves
4

Prep
15 minutes

Total
15 minutes

A classic combination of cured ham and melon is taken to the next-level in this voluptuous dish, pairing nutty, melt-in-your-mouth Jamón Ibérico with ripe cantaloupe and a fresh lemon herb salad. The combination brings out new flavors in each of its components for a palate-pleasing summer masterpiece that gets guests talking.

On the night we premiered this dish at Boqueria SoHo it caught one regular guest's attention, and he ordered it. Before he was through, he ordered another. The very next night he was back on his stool at the counter. He had been thinking about the dish all day and had to return for more! We hope you and your guests will feel the same way.

---

1 ripe cantaloupe (about 14 ounces) cut in 8 wedges and seeded
2 ounces very thinly sliced Jamón Ibérico
½ lemon
1 cup packed torn frisée
2 tablespoons fresh mint leaves, torn
2 tablespoons fresh basil leaves, torn
extra-virgin olive oil: a generous drizzle
fleur de sel
kosher salt and freshly ground black pepper

Peel the rind off the melon wedges, then slice each wedge lengthwise in half. Arrange 4 slices on each of the serving plates and drape the jamón all over the melon.

Remove the zest from the half lemon and reserve it, then squeeze out the juice. Toss the frisée, mint, and basil with the lemon juice and a pinch of salt. Mound this on top of the jamón and melon. Drizzle with plenty of oil, grind lots of pepper on top, and sprinkle with fleur de sel. Sprinkle the reserved lemon zest on top. Serve immediately.

Chef's tip: *Never put a melon in the fridge. Its sweetness and complexity diminish in the cold. If you bought it ripe, use it right away. Otherwise, let it sit at room temperature until you can smell its honeyed scent.*

ENSALADA DE COGOLLOS CON ATÚN

Tuna and Little Gem Lettuce with Piquillo Anchovy Vinaigrette

Serves
4

Prep
30 minutes

Total
30 minutes

4 jarred piquillo peppers, drained
   and finely chopped
10 anchovies, very thinly sliced
   and drained
¼ cup sherry vinegar
½ cup extra-virgin olive oil
4 Little Gem lettuces or small
   romaine hearts
7 ounces canned bonito tuna in olive
   oil, preferably ventresca, flaked into
   large chunks
1 shallot, sliced paper-thin on a
   mandoline, rings separated
2 tablespoons torn fresh flat-leaf
   parsley leaves
kosher salt and freshly ground
   black pepper

It's no wonder, given how delicious savory jarred tuna and anchovies taste with lettuce hearts known as "cogollos," that this salad is a staple all over Spain. At Boqueria, we add piquillos to provide a mild sweetness that pairs nicely with the salty fish. To ensure that every bite has some of the tender red peppers and succulent anchovies, we swirl diced bits into the dressing. The vinaigrette runs between the leaves of the quartered lettuces and all over generous chunks of tuna, infusing them with a fresh taste of Spain.

Mix the piquillos, anchovies, vinegar, and oil in a small bowl until well mixed. Season to taste with salt and pepper.

Trim off the very ends of the lettuce stems, leaving most of the stem intact so the leaves stay in place. Cut each head in quarters lengthwise and put the quarters in a large bowl. (If you prefer your lettuce to be crunchier you can also trim off the soft green tops of the leaves.) Cover with cold water and swish to remove all the grit. Lift out and dry well in a salad spinner or with paper towels. Divide among serving plates.

Scatter the tuna, shallot, and parsley over the lettuces and sprinkle with salt and pepper. Spoon the vinaigrette all over and serve immediately.

Ensalada de Alcachofas (page 80)

ENSALADA DE ALCACHOFAS

Arugula with Fried Artichokes and Spicy Mayonnaise Dressing

Serves
4

Prep
45 minutes

Total
1 hour

The town of El Prat on the outskirts of Barcelona is home to the city's airport, but what most travelers don't realize is that the scrappy fields they see stretching out from the runways to the Mediterranean coast grow Spain's best artichokes. Prized throughout Catalonia, the artichokes of El Prat find their way into many typical dishes. In Barcelona's tapas bars, they are most often served fried. The wedges of artichoke heart, browned crisp around the edges and tender inside, come with lemon wedges and a rainfall of salt. Here, this classic preparation finds a refreshing compliment in peppery arugula, nutty Mahón cheese, and a garlicky allioli dressing. A final scattering of mint leaves and lemon zest bring a bright pop to each bite.

---

1 small bunch of parsley, stems only
3 artichokes
extra-virgin olive oil
6 cups baby arugula
¼ cup Spiced Allioli Dressing
   (see page 273)
2 ounces aged Mahón cheese, shaved
   with a vegetable peeler
½ lemon, zest removed and retained
2 tablespoons fresh mint leaves
kosher salt

Place the parsley stems in a bowl of cold water; this will be used to prevent the artichokes from discoloring.

Trim the leaves and stem of each artichoke in turn. First place the artichoke on its side on the work surface and, using a bread knife, trim the stem to about 1 inch. Now turn the artichoke so that the stem is pointing away from you and, still using the bread knife and a sawing action, cut away the tough outer leaves around the widest part, rotating the artichoke as you go with your free hand and taking care not to cut too deeply; you want to save all of the white heart for the salad. Next, make a straight cut across the top, 1–2 inches down, to remove the upper leaves. Use your hands to pull off any remaining leaves around the bottom. Finally, use a paring knife to cut off the dark green outer layer of the stem and base, stopping at the white part. Dip the artichokes in the parsley water.

Use the paring knife to cut the artichoke in half from top to bottom. Cut each half in quarters, forming 8 wedges in total, each with a portion of the stem intact. Cut out the fuzzy choke from each piece and discard it. Immerse the artichoke in the parsley water and leave it there while you trim the remaining artichokes. When all the artichokes have been cut, drain the wedges well and pat dry with paper towels.

Fill a large skillet with oil to a depth of ¼ inch. Heat the oil over medium-high heat until hot but not smoking. Generously salt the artichoke sections and add to the hot oil in a single layer, working in batches if necessary. Fry, turning occasionally, until golden brown and crisp, about 8 minutes. Drain on paper towels.

Combine the arugula, allioli dressing, and half of the cheese in a large bowl. Squeeze a little lemon juice on top and season with salt. Toss until well-coated. Divide the arugula among 4 serving plates and top each with 6 artichoke wedges and the remaining cheese. Sprinkle the lemon zest over and tear the mint leaves on top. Serve immediately.

ENSALADA ROMANA

Romaine, Mint, and Hazelnuts with Romesco Dressing

Serves
2 to 4

Prep
25 minutes

Total
35 minutes

¼ cup Romesco (see page 276)
2 tablespoons sherry vinegar
2 tablespoons extra-virgin olive oil
2 heads romaine lettuce
¼ cup skinned hazelnuts, toasted and
   coarsely chopped
4 sprigs mint
2 ounces Idiazabal cheese, finely grated
kosher salt

This "Catalonian Cesar" features a dressing created by thinning our thick Romesco sauce (see page 276) with olive oil and sherry vinegar. Romaine leaves are coated in the rich, nutty dressing and hidden under a cloud of smoky Idiazabal cheese. We toss on a confetti of torn mint leaves and crushed hazelnuts to add some crunch and fresh notes. Top with boquerones for a closer spin toward a Cesar or add grilled steak or seared shrimp to turn it into a hearty lunch.

Whisk the romesco, vinegar, oil, and a pinch of salt in a large bowl. Trim the soft green tops off the lettuce and reserve for another use. Separate the leaves and place in the bowl with the romesco dressing. Toss with your hands until all the leaves are evenly coated. Transfer to serving plates.

Scatter the hazelnuts over the lettuce, then tear the mint leaves off the sprigs and scatter them on top. Finish with just enough grated cheese to cover the leaves. Serve immediately.

Ensalada Romana (page 81)

ENSALADA DE JUDÍAS

White Beans and Radicchio with Sherry Vinaigrette

Serves
8

Prep
45 minutes

Total
1 hour 45 minutes

4 cups White Beans, well drained
(recipe follows)
12 celery stalks, thinly sliced at an
angle, plus ½ cup celery leaves
1 cup fresh torn flat-leaf parsley leaves
1 radicchio, quartered, cored, and cut
into 1-inch-thick slices
1 small red onion, quartered and very
thinly sliced
2 ounces aged Mahón cheese, shaved
with a vegetable peeler
1 cup Vinagreta de Jerez (see page 270)
1 lemon, cut in wedges
kosher salt and freshly ground
black pepper

Our take on a Spanish white bean salad balances the creamy beans with crunchy celery, pleasantly bitter radicchio, parsley, and tangy Mahón cheese. We start with a foolproof technique for simmering dried beans so they end up evenly tender throughout. You can cook the beans a day or two ahead of time so you can throw the salad together in under 15 minutes. It's great for a light lunch with Pan con Tomate (see page 47).

Combine the beans, sliced celery and celery leaves, parsley, radicchio, onion, and cheese in a large bowl. Season with salt and gently toss. Add the sherry vinaigrette and a squirt of lemon juice and gently toss until evenly coated.

Divide among serving plates and grind pepper on top and, if you like, serve with lemon wedges.

White Beans

Makes about 4 cups
Prep 10 minutes
Total 3 hours, plus overnight soaking

2 cups dried white beans, such as
Ganxet (Catalan), great northern or
cannellini, picked over for stones
½ carrot, peeled
1 small celery stalk
¼ white onion
3 black peppercorns
1 dried bay leaf

Put the beans in a large bowl and add enough cold water to cover by 2 inches. Soak overnight.

Transfer the beans to a large saucepan and add the carrot, celery, onion, peppercorns, and bay leaf. Add enough extra water to cover the solids by ½ inch. Bring to a boil over high heat, then add 1 cup cold water.

Reduce the heat to low to maintain a steady, gentle simmer. Leave to simmer, adding more cold water if the liquid drops below the solids, until the beans are tender, about 1 hour. If using immediately, drain well. Otherwise, transfer the beans with the cooking liquid to airtight containers and refrigerate for up to 3 days. Drain well when ready to use, discarding the vegetables and spices.

BOQUERIA

ENSALADA DE TOMATES

Heirloom Tomatoes with White Gazpacho Dressing

Serves
1 or 2

Prep
30 minutes

Total
30 minutes

1 cup cherry tomatoes, halved
2 heirloom tomatoes (about 8 ounces
   each), cored and cut into
   1-inch chunks
1 tablespoon torn fresh basil
1 tablespoon torn fresh dill
2 pickled scallions, each cut in
   3 pieces (see page 270)
1 tablespoon sherry vinegar
2 tablespoons extra-virgin olive oil
2 tablespoons Ajo Blanco dip
  (see page 114)
1 tablespoon fresh lemon juice
1 teaspoon sesame seeds, toasted
kosher salt

Here we turn our creamy Ajo Blanco dip (see page 114) into a silky dressing by whisking in some lemon juice and a bit of water. We drizzle the garlicky sauce over vine-ripened heirloom tomatoes and torn herbs for a refreshing but filling summer salad with a rich almond-laced flavor.

Combine both kinds of tomatoes with the basil, dill, and pickled scallions in a large bowl. Season to taste with the vinegar, oil, and salt, gently tossing to mix well. Divide among serving plates.

To make the dressing, whisk the ajo blanco dip with the lemon juice, adding 1 tablespoon water if necessary, to loosen it to the consistency of creamy salad dressing. Drizzle all over the salad. Sprinkle with sesame seeds and serve.

ENSALADA DE HINOJO Y PERAS

Fennel and Pears with Fried Walnuts and Citrus Dressing

Serves
4

Prep
10 minutes

Total
15 minutes

1 tablespoon extra-virgin olive oil
²/₃ cup walnut halves
1 fennel, bulb cored and sliced a scant
  ¹/₈-inch-thick
1 small Bosc pear, halved, cored, and
  sliced a scant ¹/₈-inch-thick
2 ounces aged Manchego cheese,
  crumbled into roughly
  ½-inch chunks
fresh basil leaves, torn, about 5
  or to taste
5 tablespoons Vinagreta de Cítricos
  (see page 272)
kosher salt and freshly ground
  black pepper

Come fall, we stalk the Greenmarket in Union Square for peak-season fennel. Slightly sweet, with a crisp crunch and an anise aroma, it's delicious in this salad with ripe pears, olive oil-fried walnuts, and hand-crumbled chunks of Manchego cheese.

Heat the oil in a small skillet over medium-low heat. Add the walnuts and toss continuously to coat evenly with the oil and to toast, about 1 minute. Generously season with salt, then transfer to paper towels to drain excess oil and to cool.

Toss the sliced fennel and fennel fronds, pear, cheese, and basil with the vinaigrette, plus a pinch of salt and pepper to taste, until everything is evenly coated. Taste and add more salt if needed.

Transfer to serving plates and top with the walnuts. Serve immediately.

EGGS

EGGS

As you read this, eggs are being cracked all over Spain. Most of them will be whipped and flipped into tortilla Española, the iconic potato omelet that fuels the nation. Some will be fried and served over piles of potatoes and smoky chorizo. They will be deviled and poached and baked and added whole to rustic stews of every kind.

In Spain, eggs are a staple at the midday meal and at dinner. Most Spanish markets still source their eggs locally, and the quality can be seen and tasted. The fresh eggs have firm whites and deeply colored yolks, and pack enough flavor to make them the star of any dish.

Our favorite egg dishes here all rely on sourcing the best eggs we can find, the fresher the better. Luckily, excellent organic eggs are available at farmers' markets everywhere, and most supermarkets now carry high-quality free-range farm eggs.

Tapas 24, Barcelona, Spain

TORTILLA ESPAÑOLA

Potato and Onion Omelet

Serves
8

Prep
15 minutes

Total
45 minutes plus 15 minutes to cool

What should a Spanish tortilla be? Chefs and cooks throughout Spain have been debating this question for centuries. Some argue it should be nothing more than oil-cooked potatoes in a thick egg omelet. Others demand onions. Some keep the center runny, others cook it hard.

At Boqueria, we fall in the onion camp with almost-runny eggs. We're also in the camp of flipping the tortilla often as it cooks to give it a better shape and color, and a more even texture throughout. The technique may seem intimidating, but it's easy once you get the hang of it. In Spain, it's the first dish most kids learn to make at home. If they can do it, you can do it. Once it's done, you have a great main course. All you need to round out the meal is Pan con Tomate (see page 47), olives, bread, and a salad if you'd like. It's great on its own, but even better with a dollop of Allioli (see page 273).

2½ pounds Yukon Gold potatoes (about 8 medium), peeled and cut into ⅓-inch-thick half-moons

8 large eggs

2 cups extra-virgin olive oil

½ jumbo sweet Spanish onion, peeled and cut lengthwise in half, then in half again, so you have 4 sections, then half each again so you have ½-inch-wide julienne slices

kosher salt

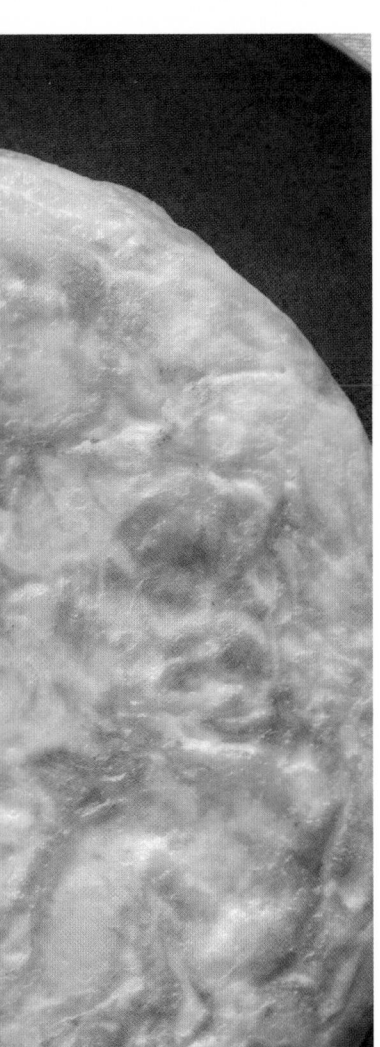

Rinse the potato slices in cold water to remove excess starch and prevent the slices from sticking when cooking. Drain, then spread on paper towels to dry completely.

Whisk the eggs in a very large bowl with a generous pinch of salt until well blended. Let stand until ready to use, about 15 minutes.

Heat the oil in a 12-inch nonstick skillet over medium-high heat until almost smoking, about 4 minutes. If you touch a potato to the oil, it should sizzle immediately. Remove the skillet from the heat and carefully add all of the potatoes. The pan will be very full.

Put the pan back on the heat. Turn the heat to high, salt the potatoes very generously, and gently and carefully stir them a little to make sure they're all submerged in the oil. When the oil comes to a boil, about 2 minutes, very carefully add the onion, gently pushing it all into the oil. Turn the heat to medium-high and cook, very carefully, gently stirring occasionally, until the onions are translucent and a paring knife easily pierces a potato, about 15 minutes. The potatoes should be tender, but not soft and mushy. It's okay if they brown a little, but if they start to brown too much, lower the heat to medium or medium-low.

Set a large strainer over a bowl and pour the potato mixture into it. Reserve the oil for another use. Immediately transfer the hot potato mixture to the beaten eggs and gently fold until well mixed. Season with salt to taste.

Wipe the skillet clean and set it over high heat. Add 1 tablespoon of the reserved oil and swirl to coat the bottom and sides. When the oil starts to smoke, after about 30 seconds, add the egg mixture all at once. Immediately stir vigorously for about 10 seconds, then spread the egg mixture in an even layer. The edges should bubble and set immediately. When they do, reduce the heat to low. Use a silicone spatula to fold the cooked edges over the wet top around the edge of the pan, creating a ½-inch rim of cooked egg all around and setting the tortilla into a perfect round. Cook for 1 minute. Remove from the heat and center a plate larger than the diameter of the skillet over the top. Protecting your hand with a towel, grasp the handle close to the pan and place your thumb on the edge of the plate to help keep it steady; with your other hand, hold the plate tightly against the skillet, and carefully flip the plate and skillet over together. Lift off the skillet, set it back on the stove, and slide the tortilla, cooked side up, into the skillet.

Set over low heat and cook for 1 minute. Repeat the flipping and cooking until the outside of the tortilla is set and the center is soft when you press it, about 3 more flips with a minute of cooking between each. The repeated flipping gives the tortilla a nicer shape and color.

When the tortilla is done, flip it out onto a cutting board or serving dish. The tortilla will continue cooking in the residual heat of the eggs. Let it cool for about 15 minutes until it is at room temperature. Cut into 8 wedges and serve.

HUEVOS CON PISTO

Eggs Baked in Sautéed Summer Vegetables

Serves
4 to 8

Prep
35 minutes

Total
45 minutes

Pisto is a ratatouille-style stew of summer vegetables from Aragon in northwest Spain. Raw eggs are often thrown right into the pot and scrambled into the vegetables, cooking instantly in the bubbling stew.

Here, to preserve the freshness of the vegetables, we roast, rather than stew, the zucchini and swap out tomato sauce for chopped tomatoes. To showcase the eggs, we avoid scrambling them in and opt for letting them poach intact to runny perfection right within the saucy mixture. A dollop of spicy pimentón yogurt adds a cooling creaminess.

This easy yet impressive one-pan-wonder is a crowd pleaser for dinner or brunch. Make sure to have plenty of good, crusty bread on hand to soak it up.

---

5 garlic cloves, thinly sliced
extra-virgin olive oil, 4 tablespoons
    plus 4 teaspoons
1 onion, cut into ½-inch dice
1 red bell pepper, stemmed, seeded,
    and cut into ½-inch dice
1 cubanelle pepper, stemmed, seeded,
    and cut into ½-inch dice
3 sprigs of thyme
2 zucchini, trimmed and cut into
    ½-inch dice
24 pieces roasted tomato quarters in
    oil, preferably Divinia, drained and
    coarsely chopped (¾ cup)
8 large eggs
½ cup labneh
¼ teaspoon lemon juice
1 teaspoon hot pimentón
chervil leaves, for garnish
kosher salt and freshly ground pepper

Place a large rimmed baking sheet on the center rack of the oven and preheat the oven to 450°F.

Combine the garlic and 2 tablespoons oil in a large, deep ovenproof skillet. Set over medium-high heat and cook, stirring often, just until the garlic gets a bit of color, about 2 minutes. Add the onion, peppers, and thyme. Season with salt. Reduce the heat to medium-low. Cook, stirring occasionally, until the vegetables are soft, caramelized, and getting just a little color, about 15 minutes.

Meanwhile, toss the zucchini with 2 tablespoons oil and a pinch of salt. Spread in a single layer on the hot pan in the oven. Roast until the bottoms are browned and the zucchini are crisp-tender, about 10 minutes. Transfer to the skillet and stir well.

Add the tomatoes to the skillet and stir well, then remove from the heat. Season to taste with salt and pepper.

Make 8 wells in the vegetable mixture. Crack an egg into each and sprinkle with salt and pepper. Transfer to the oven and roast until the egg whites are just set and the yolks still runny, about 9 minutes.

While the eggs cook, mix the labneh with the remaining 4 teaspoons oil and the lemon juice and pimentón. Season to taste with salt.

Divide the vegetables, eggs, and labneh mixture among serving dishes. Garnish with chervil and serve immediately.

TORTILLA VAGA
Open-Faced Omelet

Serves
1 or 2

Prep
20 minutes

Total
35 minutes

"Tortilla vaga" means "lazy tortilla." This set-it-and-forget-it substitute for the Spanish classic swaps fresh, quick cooking ingredients for the potatoes and requires no flipping. Just spread softly scrambled eggs in a skillet and top with anything tasty, from classic bacalao or chorizo to luxurious sea urchin or truffles. This springtime version uses juicy wild mushrooms, charred green onions, and silken slivers of jamón, served with a fresh tomato salad on toasts. Letting the salted beaten eggs sit for 10–15 minutes before cooking results in creamier scrambled eggs.

---

3 large eggs
2 scallions
extra-virgin olive oil for drizzling
  and pan-frying
1 small garlic clove, very thinly sliced
1½ ounces hen-of-the-woods
  mushrooms, trimmed and cut into
  2-inch pieces
1 sprig of thyme
½ teaspoon lemon juice
½ ounce very thinly sliced Jamón
  Ibérico, torn into slivers
Cherry Tomato Salad on Toast (recipe
  follows), to serve
kosher salt and freshly ground
  black pepper

Crack the eggs into a bowl, generously season with salt, and beat with a fork until well-blended and foamy, about 30 seconds. Let sit for 10–15 minutes while you prepare the remaining ingredients.

Trim the scallions, removing the root and about ¼ inch from the top. Cut off and reserve the white parts. Turn a gas burner to high. Set the green parts of the scallions on the grate over the open flame and cook, turning occasionally, until well-charred, about 1–2 minutes. Transfer to a cutting board, drizzle lightly with olive oil, and season with salt. Cut each piece into 1½-inch lengths.

Coat an 8-inch nonstick skillet with oil, add the garlic, and set over medium-high heat. Cook, stirring, until the garlic is fragrant, about 30 seconds. Add the mushrooms in a single layer, season with salt, and cook, stirring occasionally, for 2 minutes. Add the thyme and cook, stirring often, until the mushrooms are soft and golden, about 1 minute longer. Remove from the heat, drizzle with the lemon juice, and transfer to a plate. Discard the thyme.

Lightly coat the same skillet with oil and set over low heat. (The pan should still be hot.) Add the eggs and cook, stirring lightly, until scrambled but still very wet, about 1 minute. Spread the eggs in an even layer. Quickly press the mushroom mixture and charred scallions into the eggs. Scatter the jamón on top. Cook just until the eggs are barely set, about 1 minute longer. Remove from the heat.

Drizzle the mixture with oil, grind black pepper on top, and sprinkle the reserved white parts of the scallions all over. Serve hot, straight out of the pan with cherry tomato salad on toasts.

Cherry Tomato Salad on Toasts

4 cherry and Sungold tomatoes,
  quartered
3 basil leaves, sliced
1 teaspoon sherry vinegar
extra-virgin olive oil
2 Olive Oil Toasts (page 32)
kosher salt and freshly ground
  black pepper

In a small bowl mix together the tomatoes, basil, vinegar, oil, and salt and pepper. Place on top of the toasts. Serve immediately.

HUEVOS ESTRELLADOS

Crisp Fried Eggs with Potato Chips and Iberian Ham

Serves
4

Prep
35 minutes

Total
45 minutes

This dish may sound simple but the finished product is transcendent. When Marc was interviewing for the Executive Chef position at Boqueria, he prepared several of his favorite dishes at a tasting. When Yann tried this dish, he knew he had found the right person for the job. It was that good, and it still is.

This dish only has a few ingredients, but Marc coaxes a wide variety of temperatures, textures, and flavors from them. A piping hot just-fried farm egg sits on top of crisp housemade potato chips nestled in a rich truffled potato cream. We drape translucent slices of Jamón Ibérico over the egg to finish off the dish. Once on the table, a quick stab at the yolk sends it oozing through the chips and adds the final touch.

2 medium Yukon Gold potatoes
   (1 pound 2 ounces), peeled and
   cut into $\frac{1}{8}$-inch-thick slices on
   a mandoline
5 cups canola oil
4 large eggs
3 ounces Jamón Ibérico, sliced paper-
   thin and torn
Potato Purée (recipe follows)
kosher salt and freshly ground
   black pepper

Put the potato slices in a large bowl and cover with cold water. Swish the slices to lose all their starch. Removing the starch will prevent the potatoes from sticking to one another while frying. Lift the slices out of the water and into a colander. Repeat until the water is clear after swishing. Transfer the potato slices to paper towels and press until very, very dry.

Fill a large, very deep skillet with the oil. It should be about 1 inch deep; if not, add more. Heat over medium-high heat until very hot but not smoking, about 350–375ºF. The oil is ready when it sizzles if a potato slice is held in it. Add the potato slices one at a time until they're all submerged in the oil. Lower the heat to medium-low. Carefully swirl the pan to move the potatoes around so they fry evenly. Don't stir; this will cause the potatoes to break. Once the slices start to color, carefully turn them over. Once they're evenly dark golden brown, after about 8 minutes, transfer them to paper towels to drain and salt them generously. Reserve the oil in the pan.

Raise the heat under the oil to medium-high. Crack an egg into a small bowl, salt it, and slide it into the hot oil. Repeat with the remaining eggs, spacing them far apart in the skillet. Immediately spoon hot oil over the eggs as they cook. They should bubble and brown in 30 seconds. Transfer to serving dishes with a slotted spoon.

Divide the potato purée among the dishes, spooning it over the eggs. Top with the jamón and potato chips and serve immediately.

Potato Purée

Makes about 1 cup

1 medium Yukon Gold potato
   (7 ounces), peeled, quartered,
   and cut into $\frac{1}{2}$-inch-thick slices
$\frac{1}{3}$ cup heavy cream
$\frac{1}{3}$ cup whole milk
1 small sprig of rosemary
$\frac{1}{2}$ garlic clove, peeled
kosher salt

Combine the potatoes, cream, milk, rosemary, garlic, and a pinch of salt in a medium saucepan. Bring to a boil over high heat, then reduce the heat to a simmer. Cover and cook until the potatoes are soft enough for a knife to pierce easily, about 15 minutes.

Discard the rosemary. Transfer everything remaining in the saucepan to a blender and process until smooth. Keep warm until serving.

VEGETABLES

VEGETABLES

The diverse climate and terrain of Spain give cooks a staggering variety of domestic produce. Cool-weather-loving potatoes thrive in Galicia. Apple trees follow the rolling hills of Asturias and the Basque country down to the Ebro River basin, yielding first to stone fruit orchards, then to La Rioja's vineyards and Navarra's sunny fields of piquillos, artichokes, beans, and asparagus. Rice paddies and citrus. Almonds and olives. Spain grows everything—even bananas and pineapples, grown in the subtropical Canary Islands.

CALABAZA CON SOBRASADA

Roasted Acorn Squash with Crumbled Pork Sausage

Serves
2

Prep
25 minutes

Total
55 minutes

Come fall, the markets in New York fill with a wide variety of squash. Marc loves to roast them in the oven until tender and pair them with something salty or spicy to complement their natural sweetness.

A couple of years after arriving in the States, Marc adopted the American tradition of Thanksgiving dinner. Each year on the holiday, his house fills with friends, many of them also Spanish expats, and they can't help but add some Iberian touches to the American classics on the table. Stuffing gets butifarra sausage and potatoes are whipped to a fluff with fragrant extra virgin olive oil.

Marc created this dish for one of those Thanksgiving feasts a few years back and it ended up stealing the turkey's spotlight. A few days later, he added it to the market menu at Boqueria.

The recipe pairs sweet acorn squash with toasted hazelnuts and sobrasada, a soft, spreadable cured pork sausage from Mallorca. When cooked, the rich, fatty sausage releases the intense aroma of the smoked paprika that gives it its bright crimson color. We slather the cooked sobrasada over rounds of the squash, drizzle it with local honey, and shower it in toasted hazelnuts and sharp Mahón cheese. Serve it at any meal. It will steal the show, just as it did at Marc's Thanksgiving.

---

1 acorn squash, trimmed, cut into
  ½-inch rounds, and seeded
extra-virgin olive oil, about
  2½–3 tablespoons
½ ounce coarsely chopped
  toasted hazelnuts
2 ounces sobrasada sausage,
  skin removed
½ ounce aged Mahón cheese
2 teaspoons honey
kosher salt

Preheat the oven to 400°F.

Place the squash on a half sheet pan; generously drizzle with oil and sprinkle with salt. Toss until evenly coated. Spread in a single layer on the pan. Roast until the squash is browned and tender, about 20–25 minutes.

Meanwhile, toss the hazelnuts with a little salt and reserve.

Heat a small cast-iron skillet over medium-high heat. Add the sobrasada and cook, stirring and breaking the sausage into small bits, until the fat renders and the sausage sizzles and browns a bit, about 2 minutes.

Arrange the squash on a serving plate. Top with the hot sobrasada and any pan juices. Scatter the hazelnuts on top. Shave the cheese directly on top using a cheese plane or vegetable peeler, then drizzle with honey. Serve immediately.

ESPINACAS A LA CATALANA

Spinach with Garbanzos, Raisins, and Pine Nuts

Serves
4 to 6

Prep
10 minutes

Total
15 minutes

6 tablespoons extra-virgin olive oil
4 garlic cloves, very thinly sliced
¼ cup pine nuts, lightly toasted
¼ cup golden raisins
⅔ cup canned (and drained) or cooked
   dried chickpeas (garbanzos)
1 (16-ounce) bag baby spinach
2 tablespoons fresh lemon juice
1 tablespoon sherry vinegar
kosher salt

"A la Catalana" means "Catalan-style" and reflects a regional culinary tradition of mixing sweet and savory by adding dried fruits and nuts to everything from vegetables to meat. This simple spinach sauté combines raisins and pine nuts, the ideal duo for the delicate greens. We toss in a handful of chickpeas too, turning this into a satiating side dish.

Combine the oil and garlic in a large skillet. Set over high heat and cook, stirring, until the garlic becomes golden brown around the edges, about 1 minute. Add the pine nuts, raisins, and chickpeas and cook, stirring, for 30 seconds.

Add the spinach, season with salt, and cook, gently stirring, until barely wilted, about 1 minute. Remove from the heat and stir in the lemon juice and sherry vinegar. Immediately transfer to a serving dish and serve hot.

AJO BLANCO

In Córdoba, our chefs had dinner at Casa Pepe de la Judería, a local establishment that originally opened in the 1920s. Wrought-iron-clad windows and whitewashed walls frame the dining room. Sherry barrels rest behind the bar, and a beautiful patio provides a view straight up to the stars. This is Andalucía, the Spain of storybooks—flamenco, bullfighting, and Moorish palaces.

The restaurant sits just beyond the palm-filled courtyard of La Mezquita, an ornate and immense medieval mosque-turned-cathedral that dominates the old city center. Maybe it was the setting, but every dish our chefs tried that night tasted of history. Flavors unfurled to reveal a timeline of techniques and spices inherited from the conquering Moors, ingredients brought back by the conquistadors, and ingenuity driven by sporadic wars and famine.

The simplest dish served made the strongest impression. "Mazamorra," the waiter announced as he placed a unique regional specialty in front of us. They looked at the soup—white as the chilled bowl that held it and studded with sliced green grapes. Marc took a spoonful and was surprised at the thickness. He expected something like gazpacho, but this was thick, like a strained yogurt. He tasted the silky purée. Almonds. Bread. Garlic. Olive Oil. A tease of sherry vinegar. Incredibly creamy without a drop of cream.

The chefs looked at each other after that first mouthful, realizing in unison that they had tasted it before, that Marc had unwittingly created this dish at Boqueria only a month earlier. It happened when he was looking for a dip to accompany raw and pickled vegetables for a crudités platter. He had used ajo blanco, another chilled white soup from Andalucía, as an inspiration, but he made it thick enough to scoop up with vegetables. It was a sort of inspiration in reverse. Discovering that a dish he'd fashioned from culinary instincts already existed in Córdoba blew his mind and made him love the dip even more.

Crudités con Ajo Blanco (page 114)

CRUDITÉS CON AJO BLANCO

Crudités with Marcona Almond Dip

Serves
6 to 8 with 2½ cups of dip

Prep
10 minutes

Total
10 minutes

Ajo blanco is a refreshing, chilled "white gazpacho" thickened with almonds and loaded with garlic. Here, Marc makes an extra-thick version to use as a dip. It is as rich and creamy as hummus, but with the unmistakable luscious richness of Marcona almonds and olive oil. A generous shot of sherry vinegar and lemon juice brings a welcome acidity, making this the ideal start to any meal.

While it can be served with anything, Marc created this dip to accompany a crudité of spring vegetables. Choose whichever vegetables look best at the market. We especially love radicchio wedges, romaine leaves, baby carrots, radishes, celery sticks, and zucchini batons. Sometimes, we tuck the vegetables into a dish of crushed ice to keep them extra crunchy.

1½ cups roasted salted Marcona almonds
2 small garlic cloves, peeled
¼ cup sherry vinegar
2 tablespoons fresh lemon juice
1 cup water
¾ cup extra-virgin olive oil
kosher salt
crudités, for serving

Purée the almonds, garlic, vinegar, lemon juice, and water in a blender until very smooth, scraping the bowl occasionally. With the machine running, add the oil in a steady stream. Continue blending until the mixture thickens and emulsifies to the texture of hummus. Season to taste with salt. The dip can be refrigerated for up to 1 week.

Serve with cold crudités—plated with ice, if you like.

BRÓCOLI CON VALDEÓN

Roasted Broccoli with Blue Cheese

Serves
4

Prep
15 minutes

Total
30 minutes

2 heads broccoli, cut in half
4 tablespoons extra-virgin olive oil
⅓ cup walnuts
2 garlic cloves, sliced paper-thin on
  a mandoline
1 guindilla pepper or chile de árbol
2 tablespoons sherry vinegar
2 ounces Valdeón blue cheese, cut into
  ⅛-inch slices
kosher salt

Roasted broccoli florets are the perfect sponge to soak up ajillo, our favorite piping hot garlic and chili-laden olive oil. Funky Valdeón blue cheese from León adds a fragrant note to the dish and plays off the sweetness of the caramelized garlic. This easy tapa also makes a great side dish for steak or other grilled meats.

Preheat the oven to 500°F.

Toss the broccoli, 2 tablespoons oil, and a pinch of salt in a large bowl until the broccoli is evenly coated. Place the pieces cut side down on a half sheet pan. Transfer to the oven and roast until browned and crisp-tender, about 20–25 minutes.

Meanwhile, toast the walnuts in a medium skillet over high heat until golden brown and fragrant, about 3 minutes. Transfer to a large bowl.

Combine the garlic, guindilla, and 2 tablespoons oil in the skillet used for the walnuts. Cook over medium heat, stirring, until the garlic is golden brown, about 1 minute. Remove from the heat and add the sherry vinegar. Stir well.

Arrange the broccoli on serving plates and top with the cheese and walnuts. Drizzle the garlic oil on top and serve immediately.

Brócoli con Valdeón (page 115)

Olive Oil

A hallmark of Spanish cuisine is the generous use of olive oil, the go-to fat used for everything from frying to preserving. It's no wonder—Spain, after all, is the world's largest producer. The arid, temperate climate of the southern and eastern Iberian Peninsula is ideal for growing olive trees. More than 250 types of olive grow in Spain, many of which produce oil with surprising varietal character. For dressings we prefer extra-virgin Arbequina. The small olives are barely larger than a pea, but they produce a fruity and fragrant oil with hints of almond and apple.

We use blended, more heat-resistant olive oils for frying or searing, but we like to finish the food with a drizzle of extra-virgin. Peppery, herbaceous Picual is our staple for finishing savory dishes.

PATATAS CHAFADAS

Olive-Oil Mashed Potatoes

Serves
6 to 8

Prep
15 minutes

Total
45 minutes

2¾ **pounds Yukon Gold potatoes
(about 4 large), peeled and cut
into 1-inch chunks**
1 **sprig of rosemary**
2 **garlic cloves, unpeeled**
⅔ **cup extra-virgin olive oil**
kosher salt

We created these potatoes to accompany grilled octopus in our Pulpo a la
Plancha (see page 166) and they quickly became a go-to favorite. These loosely
smashed potatoes showcase the fruity deliciousness of Spanish olive oil, the real
star in this recipe. The oil adds a velvety lusciousness to each bite of comforting
creamy potatoes. As versatile as regular mashed potatoes, it can be paired with
any protein and is just as delicious on its own by the spoonful.

Put the potatoes in a large saucepan and add enough cold water to cover by
2 inches. Add the rosemary and garlic. Bring to a boil, then cover and reduce the
heat to maintain a simmer. Simmer until the potatoes are tender, about
25 minutes.

Drain well and discard the rosemary. Peel the garlic and place in a large bowl,
along with the potatoes. Smash with a fork while hot until well mashed, then
mix in the oil. Season to taste with salt and serve immediately.

ESCALIVADA

Charred Eggplant, Peppers, and Onion with Labneh

Serves
4 to 6

Prep
45 minutes

Total
1½ hours

The creation of this dish was a bit serendipitous. At a weekly chefs' meeting, Marc and crew were working on a new version of escalivada. They tried several ideas before Marc saw a tub of labneh on the counter. It was being used for a different recipe but the thought of another possibility intrigued him. He smeared the thick-as-cheese Middle Eastern yogurt on a plate and topped it with the charred vegetables and coarsley chopped herbs. It completely transformed the already delicious dish. The creamy tang of the yogurt highlights the natural sweetness of the smoky vegetables perfectly, while offering a cooling contrast to their burnished char. It was a home run and has been a top-selling dish ever since.

---

1 white Spanish onion

2 red bell peppers

2 Japanese eggplants, or small
   ordinary eggplants

1 cup labneh or full-fat thick
   Greek yogurt

4 tablespoons extra-virgin olive oil

2 tablespoons sherry vinegar

2 tablespoons fresh basil

2 tablespoons mint

2 tablespoons dill

2 tablespoons flat-leaf parsley leaves

Maldon sea salt flakes

kosher salt and freshly ground
   black pepper

Preheat the oven to 450°F. Heat a grill to high. If you haven't got a grill, set a wire rack over a gas burner and turn the flame to high.

Place the onion on a foil-lined shallow baking pan and roast until burnt outside and collapsed, 40–45 minutes. Leave to cool to room temperature.

Meanwhile turn the peppers and eggplants on the grill—or on the wire rack—until completely charred and smoky, 6–8 minutes. Transfer the peppers to a bowl, cover with plastic wrap, and let stand until cool enough to handle, 10–15 minutes. Letting the peppers steam in the bowl will make them easier to peel. Transfer the eggplants to a plate and let stand until just cool enough to handle. They will be easier to peel when warm.

Discard the outer burnt layers of the onion, then cut into ½-inch pieces. Pull the peppers in half, discard the stem, seeds, and ribs, then rub off as much of the burnt skin as possible. Cut into ½-inch pieces. Discard the eggplant stems, then gently peel off the burnt skin. Cut into 1-inch chunks. Put all the vegetables in a bowl, drizzle generously with oil and lightly with vinegar, and sprinkle with salt and pepper. Gently toss, then adjust the seasonings to taste.

Spread the labneh, or yogurt, on serving plates. Top with the escalivada and herbs. Sprinkle with Maldon salt flakes and drizzle with oil. Serve with warm pitas or naan bread.

Chef's tips: Because Japanese eggplants are long and slender, they take on smoky flavors much more readily than large, squat eggplants. They're also less likely to be bitter, which makes them especially suitable for this dish.

When peeling the charred skins off the red peppers and eggplants, avoid rinsing them. The water would dilute the flavor you've just concentrated over the fire. It's okay if there are some blackened bits left after peeling.

Labneh is available at Middle Eastern and specialty markets and many supermarkets. If you can't find it, refrigerate plain Greek yogurt in a fine-mesh sieve set over a bowl until it's almost as thick as cream cheese, about a day.

Escalivada

The word "escalivar" means to "char" or "grill" in Catalan, and that process, of scorching fresh vegetables on hot coals or an open flame, is what gives the iconic Catalan salad its distinctive smoky flavor and sweetness. Eggplant, peppers, and onions all grow in abundance in Catalonia. It's no wonder that they found their way into this delicious salad, which can be found in every home and restaurant. Next time you barbecue, take advantage of the hot grill to prepare a big batch of it. If you can, throw the veggies right into the hot coals. This results in outrageously delicious roasted veggies, which keep for 4 days in the fridge and can be added to salads, sauces, stews, and scrambled eggs.

Escalivada (page 120)

LENTEJAS ESTOFADAS CON PIMENTÓN

Braised Lentils with Smoked Paprika Dressing

Serves
4 to 6

Prep
25 minutes

Total
1¼ hours

These deeply spiced lentils, created as a saucy bed for our Bacon-Wrapped Cuttlefish (see page 177) are just as delicious on their own. The hearty stew is the perfect cold-day dish. A pimentón vinaigrette is stirred in just before serving to give the dish an enticing smoky aroma.

---

2 tablespoons extra-virgin olive oil
½ carrot, finely diced
½ celery stalk, thinly sliced
¼ large onion, finely chopped
½ leek, white and pale green parts only, cut in half lengthwise and sliced thinly
2 garlic cloves, smashed
1 dried bay leaf
2 cups Le Puy lentils, rinsed well and drained
5 cups Chicken Stock (see page 268)
Smoked Paprika Vinaigrette (recipe follows)
kosher salt

Heat the oil in a large, deep saucepan over medium-high heat. Add the carrot, celery, onion, leek, garlic, and bay leaf. Cook, stirring often, until just soft, about 3 minutes. Stir in the lentils.

Add the chicken stock and bring to a boil. Reduce the heat to low and leave to simmer, stirring occasionally, until the lentils are almost tender, about 25 minutes. Season to taste with salt.

Remove from the heat. Most of the liquid should have evaporated or been absorbed. If there's a lot of liquid remaining, carefully drain the excess, but it's okay if the lentil mixture resembles a stew.

Stir in the vinaigrette until well mixed. Serve hot.

Smoked Paprika Vinaigrette

Makes about 1 cup
Prep 5 minutes
Total 5 minutes

1 shallot, chopped
2 garlic cloves, chopped
2 tablespoons Dijon mustard
¼ cup sherry vinegar
2 tablespoons sweet pimentón (smoked paprika)
⅝ cup extra-virgin olive oil
kosher salt

Combine all of the ingredients, including a small pinch of salt, in a blender. Purée, starting on low speed and increasing to high, until very smooth. Season to taste with salt.

GAZPACHO
Chilled Tomato Soup

Makes
about 3¼ quarts

Prep
20 minutes

Total
4 hours

This iconic chilled soup comes from Andalucía where the relentless summer sun pushes temperatures to one hundred degrees Fahrenheit and above. It was the perfect lunch for field workers who would carry the soup in thick clay jugs, natural thermoses that would keep the soup cool for a refreshing mid-day meal. It is still the perfect summer dish.

Our version is blended extra smooth, emulsifying the bread and olive oil to give the mixture a creamy taste and silky texture. Cucumber cools while ripe tomatoes and peppers add a subtle sweetness balanced by the slight tang of garlic and onion and the bright pop of sherry vinegar. You can top the gazpacho with small croutons or diced watermelon, cucumber, onion, or pepper to give it a little crunch.

4¼ pounds ripe tomatoes (about 12), cored and cut into 2-inch chunks

1 red bell pepper, stemmed, seeded, and chopped

2 cubanelle peppers, stemmed, seeded, and chopped

½ red onion, chopped

2 garlic cloves, peeled

2 seedless (English) cucumbers, peeled and chopped

3 cups 1-inch torn chunks baguette

1 cup extra-virgin olive oil

6 tablespoons sherry vinegar

2 tablespoons kosher salt

Combine the tomatoes, peppers, onion, garlic, cucumbers, baguette, and oil in a very large bowl. Stir well to coat, then stir in the vinegar and salt until everything is very well mixed. Cover and refrigerate for 1–2 hours.

Pour the mixture into a blender and blend until very smooth, working in batches if necessary. For a smoother gazpacho, pour through a fine-mesh sieve. Refrigerate again until very cold.

The gazpacho can be refrigerated for up to 1 week.

MAÍZ RUSTIDO

Sautéed Corn with Hot Paprika Oil and Manchego Cheese

Serves
2 to 4

Prep
15 minutes

Total
25 minutes

1 lime
3 ears of corn, husks and silk removed
1 teaspoon hot pimentón
   (smoked paprika)
4 teaspoons extra-virgin olive oil
1 ounce aged Manchego cheese
Maldon sea salt

Our line cooks are the backbone of our kitchens—and a great source of inspiration. Since corn, while not commonly eaten in Spain, is so plentiful and delicious in North America in the summer, we wanted to find a way to feature it on the menu. We couldn't look to Spain for inspiration, so we looked to some of our line cooks and drew inspiration from their Mexican heritage.

We give the classic Mexican combination of corn with ground chilies, queso fresco, and lime a Spanish spin by swapping Manchego for the queso fresco and adding hot pimentón instead of ground chilies. Smoky and spicy, creamy and bright, this is an irresistible dish that flies off our market menu all summer.

Heat a grill to high. (As an alternative, you could use a rack set over a gas burner.)

Trim the top and bottom off the lime. Remove and reserve the zest. Slice between the membranes to release the lime segments. Reserve in a large bowl.

Grill the corn, turning to char evenly, until dark brown all over and tender, about 5 minutes. When cool enough to handle, cut the kernels off the cobs. Transfer to the bowl containing the lime segments and toss until well mixed. Divide among serving dishes.

Mix the pimentón and oil in a small bowl and drizzle all over the corn. Shave the cheese directly over the corn mixture with a microplane, then sprinkle the lime zest on top. Sprinkle with Maldon salt and serve immediately.

Chef's tip: If you don't want to grill the corn, you can turn it over the open flames of a gas burner until blackened and charred.

Jamón Ibérico

Jamón Ibérico is, hands-down, the best ham in the world. Its translucent fat-streaked slices melt in your mouth with a nutty sweetness. The contrast of the fat with the deep umami of the tender meat—heaven.

On a visit to a Jamón Ibérico cooperative in Córdoba's Valle de los Pedroches, our chefs met Rafa, a "maestro jamonero," or authority on all things ham, from production to slicing. He walked the chefs through the rolling hills of oak groves where pure-bred black Iberian pigs roam freely, eating grass and roots and scavenging for fallen acorns. For the final months of the pigs' lives, their diet will be restricted exclusively to acorns. That is what gives Jamón Ibérico its distinct nutty flavor and marbling.

The ham legs are salted for 40–60 days, 1 day for every kilo of weight, then hung from two-story-high rafters for at least another six months. Afterwards, they are moved to dry, dark cellars, where they will hang for between two and four years. The curing process slowly dries the meat, concentrating flavor, and the aging coaxes a deep nutty richness from the revered Ibérico hams.

JUDÍAS VERDES CON JAMÓN Y MELOCOTÓN

Green Beans with Iberian Ham and Peaches

Serves
2 to 4

Prep
10 minutes

Total
20 minutes

½ pound string beans, trimmed
1 tablespoon extra-virgin olive oil
1 ounce Jamón Ibérico or serrano,
  very thinly sliced and torn
1 garlic clove, very finely chopped
1 small ripe peach, cut into thin wedges
2 tablespoons fresh tarragon leaves
2 tablespoons Vinagreta de Cítricos
  (see page 272)
kosher salt and freshly ground
  black pepper

The classic Spanish duo of string beans and jamón takes on a fresh late-summer feel with the additional combination of peaches and tarragon. To keep the slender beans snappy and bright, we first dunk them in boiling water and then give them a quick turn in a skillet before adding in the sweet peaches and salty ham. Fragrant tarragon and a citrus vinaigrette tie it all together.

Bring a medium saucepan of water to a boil. Fill a large bowl with ice and water. Generously salt the cooking water, then add the beans. Cook until just past al dente, about 3 minutes. Immediately transfer the beans to the bowl of ice and water. Once they are cold, drain well.

Heat a large sauté pan over high heat. Add the oil and swirl to coat the bottom of the pan. When it's smoking, add the green beans and season with more salt to taste. Cook, stirring often, until tender and browned in spots, about 3 minutes.

Add the jamón and garlic. Cook, stirring, until the garlic is fragrant, about 1 minute. Season with pepper, then transfer to a large bowl.

Add the peach wedges, tarragon, and vinaigrette. Toss until well coated and season to taste. Serve immediately.

RICE & NOODLES

RICE & NOODLES

No Spanish dish captures the imagination more than paella. If you are not from Spain, everything about the dish feels exotic: the wide, shallow pan; the saffron-laced rice; the head-on shrimp, clams, and mussels. But to a Spaniard it's comfort food, a communal dish to be shared at family gatherings.

Although the dish has its roots in Valencia, where natural wetlands were first converted to rice paddies in the eighth century, variations on the classic paella and other rice dishes cooked using the same technique are as diverse as Spaniards themselves.

Mountainous regions give us rice dishes built with foraged mushrooms and wild game, while seaside towns might mix in squid ink for a black rice, rich with salty sea flavor. Along the Catalan coast, where tradesmen arrived long ago with pasta-making traditions from Italy, small fideo noodles often stand in for rice in a paella, a regional favorite known as fideuà.

At Boqueria we recommend one of our paellas to almost every table. A meal that starts with a few tapas and ends with a big satisfying pan of paella is hard to beat. When one of these showstoppers arrives at the table, everyone grabs their phones to get a picture. The dishes in this section will do the same for your guests. They taste even better than they look and make the perfect grande finale for your Spanish feast.

FIDEUÀ NEGRA

Shrimp, Clams, Cuttlefish, and Fideo Noodles with Squid Ink

Serves
4

Prep
30 minutes

Total
45 minutes

This squid ink and toasted noodle paella is one of our all-time favorites. Try it and you'll understand why.

Once on the table you'll want to grab a spoon, crack through the crispy top and mix the allioli evenly throughout the inky paella until it's as creamy as a risotto. Scrape up the crunchy base, getting plenty of the gooey center's sweet seafood and tender noodles.

It's easy to recreate this addictive dish at home. If you already have stock, sofrito, and picada, it comes together fast. You'll know it's ready when the short, thin noodles on top curl and rise like they're dancing.

2 cups fideo #1 noodles

3 cups Lobster Stock (see page 269)

2 tablespoons squid ink

extra-virgin olive oil, as needed for
frying and drizzling

12 large shrimp, peeled and deveined

12 manila clams, cleaned well

6 ounces cuttlefish, cut into
½-inch pieces

¼ cup Sofrito (see page 272)

3 tablespoons Picada (see page 274)

flat-leaf parsley leaves, for serving

Allioli (see page 273), for serving

kosher salt

Position a rack in the center of the oven. Preheat to 400°F.

Spread the noodles on a half sheet pan. Bake on the center rack, stirring once or twice, until golden brown, about 5–6 minutes. Reserve.

Meanwhile, mix the stock and squid ink in a large saucepan. Bring to a boil, then adjust the heat to maintain a steady simmer.

While the stock comes to a simmer, coat a 16–18-inch paella pan with oil. Heat over high heat until the oil is almost smoking. Season the shrimp with salt and add in a single layer. Cook only until lightly browned, about 30 seconds per side. Quickly and immediately transfer to a plate. You just want to leave some shrimp flavor in the pan; you don't want to risk overcooking the shrimp.

Turn heat to medium-high; coat the pan with oil again, add the clams, and season them with salt. Cook, shaking the pan occasionally, until they start to gape open a little (discard any that fail to open), about 2 minutes. Immediately transfer to a bowl.

Coat the pan with oil again. Season the cuttlefish with salt and add to the hot oil in a single layer. Cook, turning occasionally, until golden, about 5 minutes. You want the cuttlefish to caramelize a bit in the pan; add more oil if any pieces stick. Add the sofrito and picada and stir until well mixed. Add the toasted noodles and stir until well combined. Add the simmering stock-squid ink mixture. It should boil immediately. Season to taste with salt.

Boil the mixture over high heat for 5 minutes, then lower the heat to simmer for 5 minutes more.

Scatter the shrimp and clams and all their reserved juices on top of the cuttlefish and noodles. Cook over a low heat until the mixture is dry, about 5 minutes.

Turn the heat to high. Cook until you can hear the noodles crackling and creating the soccarat crust on the bottom, about 30 seconds. Top with parsley, drizzle with olive oil, and serve immediately with allioli.

Chef's tip: Squid ink is available in specialty stores and seafood markets.

Fideuà

Catalonia has always stood at a crossroads for trade. Over the centuries influences from across the Mediterranean have crept into the Catalan culture and pantry. One of the most easily recognized of these influences is pasta. Catalans have long incorporated it into their cuisine. Everyone makes canelones (cannelloni), pasta sheets stuffed with ground meat and baked in béchamel, and short, thin noodles often stand in for rice in paella.

To make fideuà, the popular pasta version of paella, the short vermicelli-like strands are toasted to a golden brown, then simmered in a paella pan with seafood and stock. The dish is usually served with a hefty dollop of allioli. This is stirred into the noodles before plating, mixing with any remaining stock to create a creamy sauce that sticks to the al dente pasta.

Fideuà Negra (page 138)

PAELLA MIXTA

Chicken and Seafood Paella

Serves
4

Prep
1 hour

Total
1½ hours

This "mixta" style of paella—cooking both meat and seafood into rice—is what most people outside of Spain know and love because it's delicious, homey, and incredibly satisfying. Below is a winning combination that we created after a trip to our local market. Stick to it or swap in similar ingredients; that's the spirit of "mixta." It's not just that cooks everywhere have their own versions, but they have different versions every time they make it based on whatever looks good at the market.

---

3 cups Chicken Stock (see page 268)
4 tablespoons extra-virgin olive oil
5 ounces boneless skinless chicken
   legs and/or thighs, cut into
   ½-inch chunks
5 ounces pork belly, cut into 1- by
   2-inch pieces
4 ounces cuttlefish or squid, cut into
   ½-inch dice
½ onion, very finely chopped
3 garlic cloves, minced
½ cubanelle pepper, cut into
   ½-inch squares
½ red bell pepper, cut into
   ½-inch squares
2 globe artichokes, prepared (see page
   80), each heart cut into 8 wedges
1 tomato, grated on a box grater,
   skin discarded
¼ pound green beans, preferably
   Romano beans, trimmed and cut into
   2-inch lengths
1½ cups bomba rice
2 cups broccoli florets
8 mussels, beards removed, cleaned
   well (discard any that have opened)
kosher salt and freshly ground
   black pepper

Bring the chicken stock to a boil in a large saucepan. Reduce the heat to keep just warm until ready to use.

Heat 3 tablespoons oil in a 16-inch paella pan over high heat. Season the chicken and pork with salt and pepper and put into the hot oil in a single layer. Reduce the heat to medium-high. Cook, stirring occasionally, until well-browned, about 7 minutes. Add the cuttlefish and raise the heat to high. Cook, stirring, until browned, about 3 minutes.

Reduce the heat to medium-high. Add the onion and cook, stirring, until tender and browned, about 5 minutes. Add the garlic and stir for 30 seconds, then add the peppers and season with salt. Cook, stirring often, until crisp-tender, about 5 minutes.

Add the artichokes, season with salt, and cook, stirring often, for 2 minutes. Add the tomato and cook, stirring, until the pan is dry, about 3 minutes. Add the green beans and cook, stirring, for 1 minute.

Add the hot chicken stock. Bring to a boil over high heat and season to taste with salt. Sprinkle the rice evenly in the pan. Stir it a little to make sure it's evenly distributed and submerged in the liquid, but then don't touch it again. You don't want to activate the starches and make the mixture creamy like a risotto. You want the grains to cook separately from each other. Scatter the broccoli on top. Bring to a boil over high heat and boil vigorously for 5 minutes.

Simmer until the rice is al dente, about 10 minutes. Tuck the mussels into the rice. Drizzle the remaining tablespoon oil over the rice and raise the heat to high. Cook until all of the liquid evaporates and the rice forms the soccarat crust on the bottom of the pan, about 5 minutes. Remove from the heat and cover with a clean kitchen towel. Let rest for about 5 minutes. Uncover and serve directly from the pan, discarding any mussels that haven't opened.

PAELLA DE MARISCOS
Seafood Paella

Serves
4

Prep
45 minutes

Total
1¾ hours

Crackling top and bottom, succulent goodness in the center: that's our seafood paella. We do it Catalan-style, adding both sofrito and picada for a more robust flavor. The former brings the earthy sweetness of caramelized tomatoes, onions, and garlic; the latter delivers the fresh bite of parsley in a saffron-scented olive oil. Lobster stock deepens the from-the-sea juiciness of cuttlefish, squid, mussels, clams, and cod. A lot of our diners tell us it's the best paella they've ever had anywhere in the world. Follow this simple formula and you'll hear the same when you serve it at home.

---

4 cups Lobster Stock (see page 269)

5 tablespoons extra-virgin olive oil, plus more if needed

4 ounces monkfish or cod, cut into ½-inch slices

6 large shell-on, head-on shrimp, preferably red shrimp

¼ pound cuttlefish, cut into ½-inch dice

7 ounces squid bodies and tentacles, bodies cut into ½-inch rings

3 tablespoons Sofrito (see page 272)

3 tablespoons Picada (see page 274)

1½ cups bomba rice

12 mussels, beards removed, cleaned well (discard any that have opened)

12 manila clams or cockles, scrubbed well (discard any that have opened)

kosher salt and freshly ground black pepper

Bring the lobster stock to a boil in a large saucepan. Reduce the heat to keep warm until ready to use.

Heat 2 tablespoons oil in a 16-inch paella pan over high heat. Season the monkfish and shrimp with salt and pepper and put in the hot oil in a single layer. Cook until well seared and browned, turning once, about 3 minutes. Transfer to a plate.

Heat another 2 tablespoons oil in the pan. Add the cuttlefish and squid to the hot pan in a single layer, season with salt, and stir well. If the pan is dry, add another tablespoon oil. Cook, stirring occasionally, until nicely seared, browned, and popping, about 5 minutes.

Add the sofrito and cook, stirring, then reduce the heat to low and stir in the picada. Add the hot lobster stock and raise the heat to high. Bring to a boil and season to taste with salt. Sprinkle the rice evenly in the pan. Stir it a little to make sure it's evenly distributed and submerged in the liquid, but then don't touch it again. You don't want to activate the starches and make the mixture creamy like a risotto. You want the grains to cook separately from each other.

Bring to a boil over high heat and boil vigorously for 5 minutes. Reduce the heat to low and simmer until the rice is al dente, about 10 minutes.

Tuck the mussels, clams, shrimp, and fish into the rice, evenly spacing them around the pan. Drizzle the remaining tablespoon oil over the rice and raise the heat to high. Cook until the mussels and clams open (discarding any that don't), all of the liquid evaporates, and the rice forms the socarrat crust on the bottom of the pan, about 5 minutes. Remove from the heat and cover with a clean kitchen towel. Let rest for about 5 minutes. Uncover and serve directly from the pan.

Chef's tip: If you can't find cuttlefish, also called sepia, you can use more squid instead.

Paella de Mariscos (page 144)

Paella

Over a thousand years ago, the Romans set up a rudimentary system of irrigation in the wetlands of Valencia. Three hundred years later, the Moors refined the system and introduced rice. Since then, Valencia's marshlands have supplied the country with the grain. And just as rice spread from its Valencian home, so did paella, eventually becoming the national dish.

And as with all of the country's most popular dishes, a heated debate persists about paella.

"Yes, it should have onions!"

"No, never chorizo!"

"Your mother adds the rice when?!"

"What type of rice?!"

Engaged couples have even been known to fight over which of Spain's two principal types of rice to throw at their wedding. Bomba or calasparra?

Yes, the great paella dispute can leave Spaniards simmering. But the grain of truth revealed by this ongoing debate is that everyone feels extremely passionate about paella. That includes us.

Paellera

To make a proper paella, you need a paella pan. We recommend the traditional carbon steel *paellera*, which conducts heat quickly and evenly and produces the perfect *socorrat*, the badge-of-honor caramelized base that distinguishes a perfectly executed paella. You will need to season your paella pan with oil after washing to prevent rust.

We put paella pans to all sorts of uses in the restaurant. We use them to roast whole fish or large cuts of meat and have even filled them with crushed ice to be used as impromptu platters for crudités or oysters.

ARROZ DE CODORNIZ

Quail and Porcini Mushroom Rice with Artichokes

Serves
4

Prep
45 minutes

Total
1¾ hours

4 cups Chicken Stock (see page 268)

4 tablespoons extra-virgin olive oil, plus more if needed

4 quail, each cut into 2 legs and 2 breast halves with wings attached

3 large artichokes, prepared (see page 80), hearts cut into 8 wedges

5 porcini, preferably frozen and thawed, halved lengthwise, then cut crosswise into ¼-inch slices

7 garlic cloves, sliced ⅛-inch thick

2 cubanelle peppers, cut into ½-inch squares

1½ cups bomba rice

kosher salt and freshly ground black pepper

This is our favorite winter paella. We love the creaminess of the rice against the umami of porcini mushrooms, the gaminess of quail, and the fresh bite of artichokes and peppers.

Marc created this dish from his memories of cooking at Can Jubany restaurant. West of the Mediterranean and south of the Pyrennes, Can Jabuny sits on the plains of the tiny town of Vic. Chef Jubany likes to put the surrounding fields on the plate, which means lots of wild game, foraged mushrooms, and homegrown vegetables. This paella sums up that delicious philosophy.

Bring the chicken stock to a boil in a large saucepan. Reduce the heat to keep just warm until ready to use.

Heat 2 tablespoons oil in a 16-inch paella pan over high heat. Season the quail with salt and pepper and put in the hot oil, skin side down, in a single layer. Cook until the skin is browned, about 3 minutes. Flip each piece and cook until the meat is lightly browned, about 2 minutes. Transfer to a plate.

Add the artichokes to the hot pan in a single layer, season with salt, and stir well. If the pan is dry, add another tablespoon oil. Reduce the heat to medium and cook, turning the artichokes occasionally, until caramelized, about 8 minutes. Transfer to the plate with the quail.

Add 1 tablespoon oil to the pan and add the porcini. Season with salt, raise the heat to high, and cook, stirring occasionally, until dark brown and caramelized, about 4 minutes. Push the porcini to one side of the pan and add the garlic and peppers to the other side. Season with salt, reduce the heat to medium, and cook, stirring the vegetables and shaking the pan, until lightly browned and crisp-tender, about 3 minutes.

Return the quail legs and artichokes to the pan, along with any accumulated juices. Stir well, then add the hot chicken stock. Bring to a boil and season to taste with salt. Sprinkle the rice evenly in the pan. Stir it a little to make sure it's evenly distributed and submerged in the liquid, but then don't touch it again. You don't want to activate the starches and make the mixture creamy like a risotto. You want the grains to cook separately from each other.

Bring to a boil over high heat and boil vigorously for 5 minutes. Reduce the heat to low and tuck the quail breasts into the mixture, evenly spacing them around the pan.

Simmer until the rice is al dente, about 10 minutes. Drizzle the remaining tablespoon oil over the rice and raise the heat to high. Cook until all of the liquid has evaporated and the rice forms the soccarat crust on the bottom of the pan, about 5 minutes. Remove from the heat and cover with a clean kitchen towel. Let rest for about 5 minutes. Uncover and serve directly from the pan.

SEAFOOD

SEAFOOD

Sea cucumbers. Gooseneck barnacles. Baby eels. Sea urchin. Cod cheeks. When visiting a Spanish seafood market, make sure to have Google handy.

Spaniards love seafood and take full advantage of their geographic situation, harvesting all sorts of tasty sea creatures from the warm waters of the Mediterranean, the chilly Bay of Biscay, and the open Atlantic. But Spanish cuisine celebrates much more than exotic sea oddities. Fishmongers hawk beautiful fresh fish. Sea bass, monkfish,

sea bream, and bonito tuna end up on dinner tables daily, and it's hard to find a menu that doesn't include octopus, squid, and shrimp.

Like Spain, New York enjoys an abundance of seafood. Fresh catches arrive every morning from across the northeast, and our chefs start their day by butchering whole fish and cleaning beautiful Long Island squid. These recipes use the best of our local catch, but you can always substitute whatever is freshest in your area.

Clockwise from left: Pulpo a la Plancha (page 166); Ensalada de Judías (page 84); Caballa en Escabeche (page 191); Berberechos en Salsa de Ajo y Perejil (page 169); Sardinas a la Brasa (page 188); Calabaza con Sobrasada (page 108); Crudités con Ajo Blanco (page114)

MEJILLONES CON AZAFRÁN

Steamed Saffron Mussels

Serves
2 to 4

Prep
15 minutes

Total
20 minutes

We love steamed mussels and this version with saffron and sherry packs the rich aromatic goodness of a seafood paella into the quick and easy bistro standard. Be sure to serve this with lots of good bread for soaking up the cooking juices.

---

6 tablespoons unsalted butter

¼ cup minced shallots

2 tablespoons very thinly sliced garlic

1 teaspoon fresh thyme leaves, preferably lemon thyme

1 teaspoon loosely packed saffron

½ cup amontillado sherry

2 tablespoons Dijon mustard

1¼ pounds mussels (about 30–35), cleaned and beards removed

2 tablespoons finely chopped flat-leaf parsley

1 lemon, cut into wedges

kosher salt

Melt the butter in a large, deep skillet over low heat. When it foams, add the shallots, garlic, and thyme. Cook, stirring often, until fragrant, about 3 minutes. Add the saffron, sherry, and mustard and stir well.

Add the mussels (first discarding any that are already open), turn the heat to high, and cover the skillet. Cook, shaking the pan occasionally, until the mussels just open, 2–3 minutes. (Discard any that have failed to open.) Divide the mussels among serving dishes.

Sprinkle the parsley and squeeze lemon juice from the wedges over the mussels. Season the pan sauce to taste with a little more lemon juice and salt. Spoon all over the mussels and serve immediately with the remaining lemon wedges.

Saffron

Saffron is the dried stigmas of the crocus flowers that bloom each fall in the fields of Castilla La Mancha. Each blossom has only three stigmas, and these are picked by hand right after the flowers come up but before the petals open. That's why the sunset orange threads cost so much. But they're worth the occasional splurge. They impart a distinctive honeyed floral aroma and a unique bittersweet taste. Buy only as much as you need at one time; the fresher the saffron, the more potent the fragrance.

CRUDO DE LENGUADO CON PIPIRRANA

Cured Fluke with Tomato-Pepper Vinaigrette

Serves
4 to 6

Prep
10 minutes

Total
20 minutes

A light salt cure gives raw fluke a pleasant texture in this refreshing appetizer. We looked to Pipirrana, the Andalusian salad of diced bell peppers, tomatoes, and onions, as inspiration for the vinaigrette of finely diced vegetables, lemon juice, and olive oil. We spoon it over the quick-cured fish for a light but intensely flavorful *crudo*.

If you can't find fluke, you can use another firm, flaky white fish or mackerel fillets. Just be sure the fish is fresh and of high-enough quality to be eaten uncooked.

---

kosher salt, 1 pound (2½ cups)
1 lemon, zest and juice
1 lime, zest and juice
1 tablespoon juniper berries
1 (10-ounce) skinless fluke fillet or 2 Spanish mackerel fillets
½ cup Pipirrana Vinaigrette (recipe follows), plus more to taste
1 tablespoon tarragon leaves

Refrigerate serving plates until cold.

Mix the salt, lemon and lime zest and juice, and juniper berries in a small bowl. Spread half in a shallow dish, place the fillet(s) on top, and pat the remaining salt mixture all over the fish to cover completely. Let stand for 10 minutes at room temperature.

Remove the fish from the salt mixture, rinse under cold water, and pat dry. Cut the fish into ⅓-inch-thick slices at an angle, starting at the tail and angling the knife toward the other end of the fillet.

Place the slices on the chilled serving plates. Spoon the vinaigrette over the fish, then top with the tarragon leaves. Serve immediately.

Pipirrana Vinaigrette

Serves 1¼ cups
Prep 15 minutes
Total 15 minutes

2 Roma tomatoes, peeled, seeds and ribs removed, and finely diced
1 cubanelle pepper, stemmed, seeds and ribs removed, and finely diced
¼ red onion, finely diced
½ cup extra-virgin olive oil
juice of 1½ lemons
kosher salt

Stir the tomatoes, pepper, and onion in a bowl to mix. Stir in the olive oil and lemon juice and season to taste with salt.

Chef's tip: We use cubanelles instead of regular green bell peppers since they're less watery and more flavorful. They're readily available in many supermarkets.

CALAMARES CON PATATAS ENMASCARADAS

Grilled Squid, Potato, Kale, and Blood Sausage

Serves
4

Prep
45 minutes

Total
1 hour

Marc's first cooking job outside of his family's restaurant was at a hotel in the Pyrenees north of Barcelona. It was set on a hillside so steep that the only way to get up there was by riding a funicular, the type of cable car that inches up a railway set into the slope. The hotel's chef introduced Marc to the traditional mountain dishes of Catalonia, including trinxat. The word means "to smash" in Catalan, and that's what you do with potatoes, cabbage, and meat before mixing them in a hot skillet. Here, Marc transforms that comforting mash into a modern mix with kale and sausages and tops it all with seared squid. It's just as satisfying as the original with a welcome final pop of lemon juice.

2 lemons
4 large Yukon Gold potatoes, peeled and cut in large chunks
1 (¾–pound) bunch Lacinato kale, tough stems discarded, leaves thinly sliced
½ cup extra-virgin olive oil, plus more for frying
2 links morcilla or butifarra sausages (10 ounces), casings removed
6 garlic cloves, very finely chopped
1 pound squid
kosher salt and freshly ground black pepper

First, char the lemons. Cut them in half crosswise and heat a small skillet over high heat until very hot, about 2 minutes. Place lemons cut side down and cook until charred, about 4 minutes. Set aside.

Put the potatoes in a large saucepan and add enough cold water to cover by 2 inches. Bring to the boil over high heat, then add a generous pinch of salt. Reduce the heat to low and simmer until the potatoes are tender, about 20 minutes. Add the kale and cook for 2 minutes. Drain well in a large colander, then transfer to a large bowl.

Using a large spoon or potato masher, smash the mixture until the potatoes are coarsely mashed and everything is well mixed.

Heat the oil in a large saucepot over medium-high heat. Add the sausages and cook, stirring and breaking the meat into small pieces, until browned, about 4 minutes. Add the garlic and stir until fragrant but not browned, about 1 minute. Add the mashed potato-kale mixture and stir until well mixed, then remove from the heat. Season to taste with salt and pepper.

Meanwhile, heat a large cast-iron skillet over high heat until very hot. Toss the squid with just enough oil to coat, and season with salt and pepper. Add to the smoking-hot skillet in a single layer and cook, turning once, until nicely seared, about 3 minutes.

Slide the potato mixture onto a serving plate and top with the squid. Sprinkle with salt and serve with the charred lemons for squeezing over the squid.

Ingredients for Calamares con Patatas Enmascaradas (page 163)

PULPO A LA PLANCHA
Seared Smoked-Paprika Octopus

Serves
8

Prep
30 minutes

Total
2 hours

In Galicia, octopus and potatoes are boiled together in giant pots and then chopped into bite-sized rounds and doused with olive oil and pimentón. The resulting dish, the iconic Pulpo a la Gallega, pops up on menus all over Spain and served as a starting point for Marc when he created this octopus and potato combo.

Here, we sear tender boiled octopus in an incredibly hot pan to crisp the skin for a pleasant, almost-charred taste and texture. Our rich Olive Oil Mashed Potatoes (see page 119) provide a more refined companion than the traditional boiled variety. We drape a tentacle over the potatoes and dust the plate with a mix of sweet and hot pimentón for a smoky hit, finishing it off with a bright and crunchy fennel salad.

---

1 whole (5-pound) octopus, thawed
    if frozen
1 dried bay leaf
½ teaspoon black peppercorns
3 tablespoons extra-virgin olive oil,
    plus more for drizzling
2 tablespoons hot smoked pimentón,
    plus more for serving
2 tablespoons sweet smoked pimentón,
    plus more for serving
2 fennel bulbs, sliced paper-thin
½ cup coarsely chopped flat-leaf
    parsley leaves
juice of 2 lemons
Olive Oil Mashed Potatoes
    (see page 119)
fleur de sel

Bring a large stockpot of water to the boil. Turn the octopus upside down. Stick your finger in the hole at the base of the head where all the tentacles meet and pull out the stiff beak and discard it.

Holding the octopus by its head, dunk the tentacles into the boiling water then lift it out. Repeat two more times. In Spain, we call this process "asustar," which means "to scare." Shocking the octopus with hot water helps its skin to stay intact. Immerse the whole octopus into the boiling water and add the bay leaf and peppercorns. Cover, bring the water back to the boil, then lower the heat to maintain a steady simmer. Simmer until tender but still a little bit chewy, 1 hour–1 hour 10 minutes. The best way to test this is to cut off a tentacle, slice off a piece from the thickest part, and taste it.

Transfer the octopus to a cutting board, with the head down and the tentacles on top. When cool enough to handle, cut the tentacles from the head. Reserve the head for another use.

Heat the oil in a large skillet over high heat until almost smoking. Carefully add the tentacles in a single layer, working in batches if necessary. Be careful—the oil may pop. If it does, turn the heat to low. Cook, turning once, until deeply browned and crisp, about 8 minutes.

Remove from the heat and dust with both pimentóns, sifting the spice over the octopus through a fine-mesh sieve to coat completely.

Toss the fennel and parsley with the juice of both lemons, 2 teaspoons oil, and a pinch of salt. The mixture should taste quite acidic.

Divide the potatoes among serving plates and top with the octopus then the fennel salad. Sprinkle with fleur de sel, drizzle with olive oil, and dust with more pimentón.

Chef's tip: Look for octopus from Spain or Portugal for the most authentic flavor. If necessary, you could buy it frozen and thaw it overnight in the refrigerator.

BOQUERIA

BERBERECHOS EN SALSA DE AJO Y PEREJIL

Cockles with Garlic-Parsley Sauce

Serves

4

Prep

20 minutes

Total

25 minutes

Tucked away in Barcelona's Boqueria Market, the always-packed tapas counter at Kiosko Universal dishes up one of the best versions of clams we've ever tasted. Benja, one of the owners of Universal and a good friend of Marc, sears cockles and clams on the plancha and drizzles them with a simple garlic-parsley oil. It's a dish that Marc has always loved, and one that he brought to Boqueria. We love to prepare this dish with cockles or razor clams, but any variety will work. Find what's freshest and go from there. Cook the cockles until they open and no longer for the most succulent results.

¼ cup extra-virgin olive oil

1¼ pounds cockles, razor clams,
  or manila clams, scrubbed clean

⅔ cup Salsa de Ajo y Perejil
  (see page 274)

5 lemon wedges

2 tablespoons torn flat-leaf
  parsley leaves

2 sprigs of dill, leaves only, torn

crusty bread for serving

fleur de sel

Heat the oil in a large, deep sauté pan (with a lid) over high heat until smoking. Add the cockles, cover, and shake the pan well. Let sit until the cockles begin to open, 1–3 minutes.

Remove from the heat, uncover, and add the salsa. Swirl the pan to coat the cockles evenly with the salsa. Squeeze the juice from 1 lemon wedge on top, then divide the cockles among serving dishes. Taste a cockle and see if you need to add any salt. If so, sprinkle with a little fleur de sel.

Sprinkle the parsley and dill leaves on top of the cockles and serve with the remaining lemon wedges and crusty bread.

Chef's tip: If you can find fresh razor clams, try them here instead of the cockles—they're perfect for this recipe too.

CIGALAS A LA PARRILLA

Seared Langoustines with "Bilbaína" Sauce

Serves
4

Prep
25 minutes

Total
30 minutes

8 whole head-on langoustines
1 cup extra-virgin olive oil, plus
  more if needed
8 garlic cloves, very thinly sliced
4 small guindilla peppers or chiles
  de árbol
2 tablespoons plus 2 teaspoons
  sherry vinegar
2 cups torn frisée
flat-leaf parsley leaves, for serving
kosher salt and freshly ground pepper

Langoustines look like a hard-shelled, bright orange-red crayfish and taste like a succulent cross between the best shrimp and lobster you've ever had. To preserve their integrity, we simply sear them and top them with a garlic and chili-infused olive oil. If you can't find langoustines, you can use the sauce on the largest head-on shrimp you can find, prepared in the same way.

Prepare the langoustines: Put a langoustine on a cutting board with the head facing you, the tail pointing away in the opposite direction. Position the knife tip in the center of the head where it meets the body and bring the blade down to split the head in half lengthwise. Rotate the langoustine 180 degrees and repeat the process to split the tail in half. You should now have two lengthwise halves of a single langoustine. Remove and discard the vein. Repeat with the remaining langoustines.

Season all the cut sides of the langoustines with salt and pepper, then drizzle each with 1 tablespoon oil so the flesh is well-coated.

Combine the remaining ½ cup oil, garlic, and peppers in a small skillet and place over low heat.

Heat a very large skillet over high heat until it's smoking hot. Put the langoustines into the pan, flesh side down, working in batches if necessary to avoid overcrowding the pan. If the langoustines don't sizzle steadily in oil, add another tablespoon or two. Cook until the flesh is a nice golden brown and releases easily from the skillet, about 45 seconds, then flip them so they're shell side down. Cook until the flesh is no longer translucent, about 15 seconds more. Transfer to serving plates.

Meanwhile, when you put the langoustines into their pan, turn the heat under the garlic mixture to high. Cook, stirring occasionally, until the garlic is browned, about 2 minutes. Remove from the heat, add the sherry vinegar, and stir well.

Mound the frisée over the langoustines and top with parsley. Spoon the hot garlic dressing all over the frisée and langoustines. Serve immediately.

GAMBAS AL AJILLO

Garlicky Sautéed Shrimp

Serves
1 or 2

Prep
10 minutes

Total
20 minutes

In this irresistible tapas bar classic, fresh shrimp cook almost instantly in piping hot olive oil laced with chilies and loads of sliced garlic. We add a shot of brandy for an even deeper flavor and a hint of sweetness.

At the restaurants we cook and serve this dish in the same pan, a small cast iron skillet. When it hits the table it is still bubbling and steaming, releasing the wildly enticing aroma of caramelized garlic and briny shrimp. If you can, do the same at home, and always serve this with enough bread to soak up every last drop of the ridiculously flavorful oil.

---

6 tablespoons extra-virgin olive oil

3 garlic cloves, very thinly sliced

2 guindilla or other small hot dried red peppers, such as chiles de arbol

¼ pound medium shrimp, preferably red, peeled and deveined

1 tablespoon brandy

1 tablespoon finely chopped flat-leaf parsley leaves

1 tablespoon lemon juice

Combine the oil, garlic, and peppers in a medium skillet. Set over high heat and cook, stirring, until the garlic becomes golden brown, about 2 minutes. Add the shrimp in a single layer and cook until the undersides color, about 45 seconds. Flip all the pieces quickly.

Add the brandy. Using a long match, or carefully tilting the skillet toward the flame, flambé the brandy. Cook until the flames die out, about 30 seconds. Remove from the heat.

Top with the parsley and lemon juice and serve immediately from the skillet.

Chef's tips: If you're not comfortable flambéing the brandy, you can just let it boil for a minute instead.

If you happen to have lobster stock on hand, add this to the dish to bump up the flavor even more. Just pour in a little after the brandy and heat to a simmer. (See page 269 for our house-made stock.)

SUQUET DE PESCADORES

Monkfish, Shrimp, and Clam Stew

Serves
4

Prep
30 minutes

Total
45 minutes

This Catalonian fish stew was the traditional favorite of fishermen who used to make it right on the boat with the fish scraps they knew would not sell at the market.

This version of the humble dish tastes just as warm and comforting as the original, but does away with the odd cuts of fish for a luxurious trio of clams, shrimp, and monkfish gently cooked in lobster stock. If you have picada, sofrito, and stock on hand, you can get this hearty one-pot meal on the table in under 20 minutes.

¾ **pound fingerling potatoes (about 12–16), cooked**

¼ **cup extra-virgin olive oil**

½ **cup Picada (see page 274)**

¾ **cup Sofrito (see page 272)**

4 **cups Lobster Stock (see page 269)**

1 **pound manila clams (about 30), scrubbed**

1 **pound (about 15 or 16) large shrimp, preferably red, peeled and deveined**

1 **pound monkfish or cod fillet, cut into ½-inch slices**

finely chopped flat-leaf parsley, for serving

lemon wedges, for serving

kosher salt

Cut the potatoes lengthwise in half, then, if small, crosswise into quarters. If large, cut the halves crosswise into ¾-inch thick slices.

Heat the oil in a large cassoulet dish or heavy saucepot (minimum capacity of 3 quarts) over high heat. Add the potatoes in a single layer and sear, tossing occasionally, until browned, 1–2 minutes. Remove from the heat and pour or spoon excess oil out of the pot.

Add the picada and sofrito and set over low heat. Cook, stirring, for 30 seconds. Add the lobster stock, raise the heat to medium-high, and bring to the boil. Add the clams and stir well. Season the shrimp and fish with salt, then add to the mixture. Carefully swirl the pot to coat everything with the liquid. Simmer for 1 minute, then flip the fish and shrimp. Continue cooking and swirling the pot just until the clams open and the fish and shrimp are just opaque throughout, about 2 minutes.

Season to taste with salt and divide everything among serving bowls; top with the parsley. Serve immediately with the lemon wedges for squeezing.

SEPIA CON BEICON Y LENTEJAS AHUMADAS

Seared Bacon-Wrapped Cuttlefish with Smoked Paprika Lentils

Serves
4

Prep
25 minutes

Total
45 minutes

In late spring of 2000 Marc was wrapping up a chef gig in Barcelona and planning to retreat to his family's small vacation home on the Costa Brava for the summer. Since beginning his career as a chef, he had never taken any real time off, and he was looking forward to some down time. He would end up going to the Costa Brava that summer but under totally different circumstances than he had originally planned.

Just days before he was set to begin his summer vacation, he got a phone call from his friend Angel. "Marc! Adrià's looking for *stagiares* at El Bulli! Interested?" Marc listened as his friend explained the details of an unthinkable opportunity to intern at Ferran Adrià's revolutionary (now closed) restaurant. He couldn't pass it up and applied for the spot. He got it.

He was going to Costa Brava, to the little village of Roses that El Bulli called home. Instead of tuning out for the summer, he would be tuning in to Adrià, the maestro of the culinary world, and pushing himself to learn as much as he could while there.

One of the dishes he loved most from the menu at El Bulli that summer was sea cucumber wrapped in bacon. It was a revelation: fatty pork crunch with the soft cucumber. Marc looked to that memory to inspire this dish where he sears bacon-coddled cuttlefish strips, then nestles them in steaming smoky lentils.

---

1 whole (1-pound) cuttlefish body, well cleaned
4 slices thick-cut applewood-smoked bacon (about 6 ounces)
¼ cup extra-virgin olive oil
Braised Lentils with Smoked Paprika Dressing (see page 124)
flat-leaf parsley leaves, for serving
kosher salt

Cut the cuttlefish body lengthwise into long ⅛-inch-thick strips. Separate the strips into 8 even bunches (about 2 ounces per bunch). Cut each strip of bacon in half crosswise. Wrap one piece of bacon tightly around the center of one bunch, overlapping the ends to seal. Repeat with the remaining bunches and bacon strips.

Heat a large cast-iron skillet over high heat until very hot. Put half of the bunches in the pan in a single layer, bacon seam side down. Drizzle half of the oil over the cuttlefish. Cook, turning to sear evenly, until the outside of the cuttlefish is golden brown and the bacon is cooked through, about 6 minutes. Sprinkle the cuttlefish lightly with salt. Repeat with the remaining bunches and oil. Be sure to avoid overcooking the cuttlefish or it'll end up tough and chewy.

Divide the lentils among serving plates and top with the bacon-wrapped bunches. Garnish with the parsley and serve immediately.

El Vermut (page 180)

EL VERMUT

Spanish Seafood Platter with Salsa Espinaler

Serves
6 to 8

Prep
20 minutes

Total
20 minutes

In New York we have brunch, but, in Barcelona, lazy weekend meals are best begun with "El Vermut." This easygoing, early-afternoon tradition turns cans of preserved seafood delicacies into a hearty first course or light meal paired with an aperitif wine. On the food front, potato chips and Pan con Tomate (see page 47) round out the feast, and Barcelona local favorite "Salsa Espinaler," is the must-have condiment. It's been blended and bottled by the same century-old family company since 1950, and has been poured over canned seafood, potato chips, and olives in copious amounts ever since. We've made our own version of the "Salsa Espinaler" to accompany the dish. We keep the essence of the original but add a hit of citrus to round out the vinegar's acidity.

Re-creating this tradition stateside provides the perfect opportunity to change hearts and minds about canned seafood. Keep your pantry stocked with some cans of beautiful imported Spanish shellfish, octopus, bonito tuna, and sardines, and you will be able to pull off an impressive spread in minutes.

1x 128-gram (4.9-ounce) can mejillones en escabeche

1x 120-gram (4-ounce) can bonito del norte

1x 90-gram (3.2-ounce) can razor clams in brine

1x 200-gram (7-ounce) box boquerones

1x 138-gram (5-ounce) box berberechos

1x 350-gram (12.3-ounce) jar piparras

1x 56-gram (2-ounce) jar salt-cured anchovies

4 Brunswick sardines

1x (15-ounce) bag potato chips, preferably Spanish olive oil chips

Espinaler Sauce (recipe follows)

Open all the cans of seafood. Using a pick or fork, pull the pieces of seafood out of the liquid in the cans and arrange them decoratively on serving plates. Scatter the potato chips on top, then drizzle with the espinaler sauce. Serve immediately.

Chef's tip: To wash it down, a glass with chunky ice cubes gets a hefty pour of the vermut; the meal's star component. A generous splash of seltzer, a squeeze of lemon or orange, and an olive turn the aromatic herbal aperitif wine into a perfect hair-of-the-dog appetite-enticing cocktail.

Espinaler Sauce

Makes about ½ cup
Prep 5 minutes
Total 5 minutes

2 teaspoons hot pimentón (smoked paprika)

1 teaspoon freshly ground black pepper

1 teaspoon sugar

1 lemon

½ teaspoon kosher salt

1 garlic clove, finely grated

1 tablespoon fresh orange juice

³/₈ cup sherry vinegar

Stir together the pimentón, pepper, and sugar in a medium bowl. Zest the lemon directly into the mixture and stir again. Squeeze 2 tablespoons juice from the lemon into the bowl and add the salt, garlic, orange juice, and vinegar. Stir until the sauce is well mixed and the sugar and salt have dissolved.

The sauce can be refrigerated for up to 1 week.

Chef's tip: You can make the sauce mild by using all sweet pimentón or 1 teaspoon each hot and sweet pimentón.

LUBINA AL HORNO

Roasted Whole Branzino with Potatoes, Onion, and Peppers

Serves
2

Prep
1 hour

Total
1½ hours

Small picturesque fishing villages dot the coast of the Basque Country in northern Spain. One of the most charming of these villages is Getaria. Whitewashed buildings line the old port in the center of town where colorful fishing boats arrive each afternoon with the day's catch. In the shadow of the town's beautiful stone church, the chefs at Restaurante Kaia grill just-caught whole sea bream over live-fire grills, and top them with the classic Basque topping of bilbaína, which is essentially garlic sizzled in olive oil. At the table, you pull the meat off the bones, letting the garlicky oil mix with the sweet seawater juices of the fish.

Yes, we want to be there as much as you do right now, and that's why we created this dish, as it transports you to the seaside villages of Spain. We use branzino, a Mediterranean sea bass readily available domestically. To turn the juicy whole fish into a one-pan meal, we've cooked it over a hearty and flavorful bed of potato, onion, and peppers. We douse it all with our play on bilbaína, adding a bit of chili heat and tangy capers and sherry vinegar. It's fresh, warming, and super satisfying any time of year.

---

1 large Idaho potato, scrubbed well
    and cut into ¼-inch slices
½ onion, very thinly sliced
½ red pepper, very thinly sliced,
    or chile de arbol
½ green pepper, very thinly sliced
2 garlic cloves, very thinly sliced
extra-virgin olive oil, for drizzling
1 whole (1½-pound) branzino,
    butterflied (ask your fishmonger
    to do this for you)
¼ cup dry white wine
¼ cup Warm Ajillo Vinaigrette
    (recipe follows)
salt and freshly ground black pepper

Position two racks in the oven: one in the center and one in the lowest position. Preheat the oven to 375°F.

Combine the potato, onion, both peppers, and the garlic in a large bowl. Drizzle with oil, season with salt and pepper, and toss until evenly coated. Spread in an even layer in a paella pan. Bake on the center rack until a cake tester or paring knife slides through a potato slice easily, about 40 minutes. Remove the dish from the oven and raise the oven temperature to 500°F.

Generously season the fish with salt and pepper and drizzle with olive oil inside and out. Open the fish and place it skin side down over the potato mixture.

Place on the lower oven rack and roast for 5 minutes. Pour the wine over the fish and return to the oven. Roast until the fish is cooked through, about 5 minutes more.

Spoon the vinaigrette over the fish and serve immediately.

Warm Ajillo Vinaigrette

Makes about ⅔ cups
Total 6 minutes

½ cup extra-virgin olive oil
4 garlic cloves, very thinly sliced
2 guindilla or any spicy dried red peppers
1 tablespoon capers
3 tablespoons sherry vinegar
1 tablespoon finely chopped
    flat-leaf parsley

Combine the oil, garlic, and peppers in a small saucepan. Set over medium heat and cook, stirring, until the garlic is golden brown, about 4 minutes.

Remove from the heat and stir in the capers, vinegar, and parsley. Use immediately.

Lubina al Horno (page 181)

RAYA A LA PLANCHA
Seared Skate Wings

Serves
4

Prep
45 minutes

Total
1 hour

Skate is a flat ray fish whose "wings" or fins provide chefs with ribbed crescent-shaped fillets that cook to silky and deeply flavorful perfection. When purchasing skate, insist upon taking a whiff before your fishmonger wraps it up. Skate must be as fresh as possible; if you smell the slightest bit of ammonia, pass for a fresher cut. This version is on our market menu every winter. The skate is seared on the stove top and accompanied by caramelized rutabaga and pickled cauliflower.

---

2 boneless, skinless skate wings
   (12 ounces each), halved
extra-virgin olive oil, for cooking
Herbed Yogurt (recipe follows), to serve
Roasted Rutabaga (recipe follows)
Pickled Cauliflower (recipe follows)
kosher salt and freshly ground
   black pepper

Generously season each skate wing with salt on both sides. Fold each half in half. Because boneless skate wings are so flat, they have a tendency to overcook, so this permits the outside to brown nicely while the inside stays moist.

Heat a large skillet over high heat until very hot. Coat the bottom of the skillet with oil, then add the skate in a single layer. Add more oil if needed to have the skate sizzling steadily. Cook until the underside is very well browned, about 3 minutes. Carefully flip and cook until the center of the fish is barely opaque, 2–3 minutes more. Remove from the heat and grind black pepper on top.

Divide the herbed yogurt among serving plates and top with the seared skate and roasted rutabaga. Drain the pickles and scatter on top, along with some fresh dill leaves. Serve immediately.

Herbed Yogurt

1 cup labneh
¼ cup extra-virgin olive oil
1 rounded tablespoon minced chives
1 rounded tablespoon finely chopped
   flat-leaf parsley leaves
1 rounded tablespoon chopped dill
   leaves, plus more for serving
2½ tablespoons lemon juice or to taste
kosher salt

Mix the labneh, oil, chives, parsley, dill, and lemon juice in a medium bowl. Season to taste with salt, then add more lemon juice and/or salt to taste. Refrigerate until ready to serve, up to 6 hours.

Roasted Rutabaga

1 rutabaga, peeled, quartered, and cut
   into ½-inch slices
2 tablespoons extra-virgin olive oil
kosher salt

Place a large rimmed baking sheet on the center rack of the oven and preheat the oven to 450°F. Toss the rutabaga with the oil and a generous pinch of salt in a large bowl until evenly coated. When the oven is heated, spread the rutabaga on the hot baking sheet in a single layer in the pan. Roast the rutabaga for 15–20 minutes until browned on the undersides and tender.

Pickled Cauliflower

2 cups Pickling Liquid (see page 270)
1 head cauliflower, cored, florets cut
   into 2-inch chunks

Bring the pickling liquid to the boil. Pack the cauliflower into a jar or other airtight container. Pour the boiling liquid over the cauliflower and seal the jar. Once at room temperature, refrigerate for at least 4 hours or up to 24 hours.

BOQUERIA

La Plancha

At the heart of every Spanish restaurant kitchen is the plancha, a ripping hot flat-top grill. Its intense, direct heat caramelizes the exterior of proteins and vegetables while keeping the interior moist. A quick pass sears squid to tender perfection and plumps shrimp to an irresistible pop. It crisps the skin of fresh fish to a crackle and brands a savory crust onto meat.

The simplicity of plancha cooking makes it a go-to for cooks looking to spotlight great products with little fuss. Throw something on the plancha and dress it with a little salsa verde or romesco for an effortless stand-out meal.

Chances are you don't have a plancha at home, but a griddle or a wide, shallow pan heated to about 400°F will do the trick. The plancha is ready for use when water drops sprinkled onto the surface dance on contact. Coat what you're cooking in olive oil before throwing it on. Cooking times will vary widely depending on what you're preparing, but the goal is a brown crust outside and perfectly cooked inside.

SARDINAS A LA BRASA

Grilled Sardines with Parsley and Caper Salad

Serves
2 to 4

Prep
15 minutes

Total
25 minutes

When we think of grilled fresh sardines, we think of Málaga on the Costa del Sol in southern Andalucía. Along those stretches of soft sand, vendors line up silvery sardines like soldiers and spear them with a stick to turn them over wood fires. Slid onto a plate and topped with garlic and parsley, they're the best post-swim snack ever.

Beach or not, sardines don't get better than when they're hot off the grill. They're easy to make and even easier to eat. Hold them by the tail and pinch the filets. The moist meat just falls off the bone. Savor, and lick the dripping juices off your fingers. Repeat.

To make that little slice of heaven even sweeter, we go savory with a parsley-caper topping.

---

2 large or 4 small sardines, cleaned and gutted

4 tablespoons extra-virgin olive oil, plus more for drizzling

⅓ cup flat-leaf parsley leaves, coarsely chopped

1 tablespoon capers, drained

2 strips lemon zest (½-inch-wide and 3 inches long), removed with a vegetable peeler, torn into 1-inch pieces

juice of ½ lemon

½ garlic clove, very thinly sliced

lemon wedges, to serve (optional)

kosher salt

Heat a grill over high heat until very hot.

Season the sardines with salt and rub with the oil to coat generously. Grill until the skin releases easily from the grate, about 3–4 minutes. Carefully flip and grill just until the other side also releases, about 2–3 minutes. (You want to avoid overcooking the fish.) Carefully transfer to serving plates.

Toss the parsley, capers, lemon zest and juice, garlic slices, and a pinch of salt in a small bowl. Scatter all over the fish. Generously drizzle with oil and serve immediately, with lemon wedges on the side, if you wish.

Chef's tip: Leave the sardines on the grill until a nice crust forms on the underside. You want to get rid of as much water as possible to prevent the skin from sticking. If the skin does stick, leave it just a little longer before flipping. Don't worry; it'll be delicious no matter what.

CABALLA EN ESCABECHE

Pickled Boston Mackerel and Vegetables

Serves
4

Prep
45 minutes

Total
1 hour, plus overnight marinating

The pickling process used for canning seafood in Spain finds its roots in escabeche, a technique using a vinegar-wine-oil marinade to cook and store seafood or meat. Originally introduced by the Moors, it began as a way to extend the shelf life of perishable products. It continues to play an important role in the Spanish kitchen and we often use escabeche at Boqueria. In this dish, the light pickling method transforms fatty mackerel by giving it a firm but flaky texture and imparting a lively tang and spice that balances the rich and fatty fish. Serve this as you would a ceviche; refreshing and filling, it's the ideal dish for a warm day.

---

1 whole Boston mackerel (about ¾ pound), gutted and cleaned

²/₃ cup extra-virgin olive oil

1 head garlic, cut in half crosswise through the "equator"

½ white Spanish onion, thinly sliced

1 celery stalk, peeled to remove the tough fibers and sliced

1 large carrot, peeled and cut into ¼-inch slices

½ teaspoon black peppercorns

2 dried bay leaves

3 strips lemon zest (½-inch-wide and 3 inches long), removed with a vegetable peeler

3 strips orange zest (½-inch-wide and 3 inches long), removed with a vegetable peeler

1 cup white wine vinegar

½ cup dry white wine

2 sprigs of rosemary

kosher salt and freshly ground black pepper

Season the mackerel inside and out with salt and pepper.

Heat the oil in a large, deep skillet or sauté pan over medium-high heat. Add the garlic, cut side down. Let sit until fragrant and browned, about 3 minutes. Add the mackerel. Cook for 2 minutes, then flip over. Cook for 2 minutes more, then transfer to a plate with a slotted spatula. You want to just sear the fish at this stage and not have it cook through.

Add the onion, celery, and carrot to the oil and season with salt. Cook, stirring occasionally, for 1 minute. You don't want the vegetables to color or soften. Add the peppercorns, bay leaves, and lemon and orange zest. Cook, stirring often, for 3 minutes. Add the vinegar, wine, rosemary, and ¼ cup water. Bring to the boil and boil until the alcohol cooks off, about 3 minutes.

Bring the sauce to a simmer and return the fish to the pan along with any accumulated juices. Cover, remove from the heat, and let sit until cooled to room temperature, about 30 minutes. Transfer to the refrigerator and refrigerate at least overnight or up to 3 days. Season to taste with salt. Transfer to a serving platter, then serve cold or at room temperature.

MEAT & POULTRY

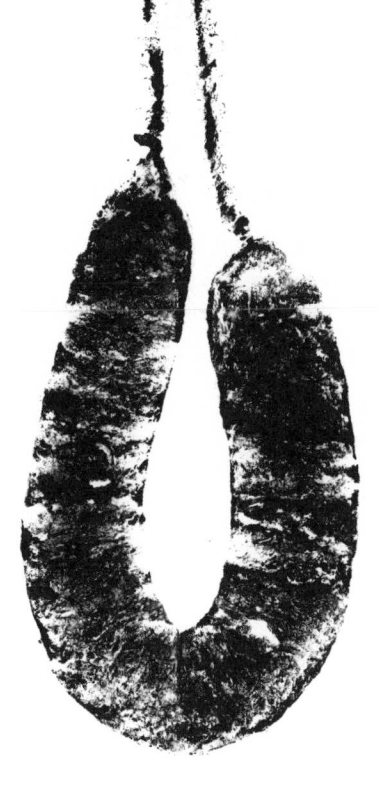

MEAT & POULTRY

We cook meat. We braise it and roast it and grill it. We simmer juicy pork meatballs and sweet red shrimp together into a succulent surf and turf. We slather big Basque-style ribeyes with smoky pimentón butter and stew tender pork cheeks with earthy chanterelles. Pork belly gets rolled up into a meaty roast and browned to a glassy crisp. Chicken and prunes are stewed to sticky fall-off-the-bone satisfaction. Our Spanish culinary heritage provides endless inspiration for hearty and homey meat and poultry dishes. We can't bring Ribera del Duero's milk-fed lamb or Segovia's suckling pig to Manhattan, but we can work with the same passion for product and careful attention to preparation that made those classics legendary.

ALBÓNDIGAS CON GAMBAS

Pork Meatballs Stewed with Shrimp and Black Trumpet Mushrooms

Serves
4 to 6

Prep
2 hours

Total
2½ hours

Silky mushrooms are draped over tender meatballs alongside succulent giant red shrimp in this hearty stew that celebrates Catalonia's *mar i muntanya* (sea and mountain) tradition. The Catalonian coast is only an hour's drive away from some of the highest peaks in the Pyrenees, so it's no wonder that the geographic proximity of the two is reflected in a culinary tradition that marries mountain and sea. This stew is arguably one of the most deeply satisfying examples of Catalonian "surf 'n' turf."

1½ cups ½ inch-cubes of country bread, crusts removed

½ cup whole milk

1½ pounds ground pork (20 percent fat)

4 garlic cloves, finely chopped and kept separately

½ cup finely chopped flat-leaf parsley leaves

1 large egg, beaten

1 cup all-purpose flour

canola or blended canola-olive oil, for frying

12 carabineiros shrimp or other jumbo head-on shrimp or crayfish (1 pound)

3 tablespoons extra-virgin olive oil

2 quarts Chicken Stock (see page 268)

½ ounce dried black trumpet mushrooms or equivalent of other wild mushrooms

2 cups boiling water

½ white onion, very finely diced

2 small carrots, peeled and diced

¼ cup canned tomato sauce

1 cup dry red wine

2 tablespoons Picada (see page 274)

kosher salt and freshly ground black pepper

To make the meatballs, put the bread in a large bowl and pour the milk over it to soak. Let stand until very soft. Mash the bread with a fork until it's in bits. Pour out any excess milk. Add the pork, 2 of the chopped garlic cloves, and the parsley, egg, and a generous pinch each of salt and pepper. Mix with your hands until everything is evenly distributed, but avoid overworking or compacting the mixture too much.

Put the flour in a shallow dish. Lightly wet or oil your hands and pinch off enough of the meat mixture to roll into a 2-inch ball. Roll this in the flour to coat and transfer to a plate. Repeat with the remaining meat mixture and flour, wetting or oiling your hands as necessary to roll smooth balls. You should have about 18–20 pork meatballs.

Fill a large saucepan with canola oil to a depth of ½ inch. Heat over medium heat until hot but not smoking. Add just enough balls to fit in a single layer without crowding. Cook, carefully turning occasionally when a golden brown crust forms, about 4 minutes. Use a slotted spoon to transfer to a plate. Repeat with the remaining meatballs. Pour out the oil and reserve for another use; reserve the saucepan.

To make the shrimp stock, separate the shrimp heads from the tails and peel and devein the tails. Reserve all the heads and shells. Refrigerate 6 heads to reserve for serving; refrigerate the prepared shrimp tails until you're ready to cook them.

Using the saucepan previously used for cooking the meatballs, heat 2 tablespoons olive oil over high heat. Add the shrimp heads and shells and a generous pinch of salt. Cook, stirring and smashing the heads and shells with a slotted spoon to release their juices, until caramelized, about 6 minutes. Add the chicken stock and bring to the boil. Reduce the heat and let simmer for 5 minutes, then reduce it further to low heat to keep the mixture just warm.

Put the dried mushrooms in a medium bowl. Pour enough boiling water over them to cover. Let stand until softened, about 15 minutes, then drain.

Meanwhile, combine the remaining 1 tablespoon olive oil and remaining chopped garlic in a Dutch oven or large, deep skillet. Cook over medium-low heat until the garlic is golden and softened, about 1 minute. Add the onion and a pinch of salt. Cook, stirring occasionally, until just softened, about 4 minutes. Add the carrots, reduce the heat to low, and cook, stirring occasionally, until the carrots are caramelized, about 25 minutes.

Add the tomato sauce and cook, stirring often, until it is reduced to a thick paste and is caramelized brown, about 6 minutes. Add the wine and bring to the boil. Boil until the sauce is thick and syrupy, about 10 minutes. Add the meatballs and any accumulated juices. Strain the hot shrimp stock into the Dutch oven to cover the meatballs, pressing on the shells to extract as much liquid as possible. Bring to the boil, then reduce the heat to maintain a low simmer. Simmer until the meatballs are cooked through, about 20 minutes.

Drain the mushrooms and stir into the mixture. Season to taste with salt. Gently fold in the picada until well mixed. Season the reserved shrimp tails and heads and tuck them into the mixture. Remove from the heat and let stand until the residual heat gently cooks through the shrimp tails and heads, about 4 minutes. Serve immediately.

Albóndigas con Gambas (page 196)

PANCETA RUSTIDA

Roasted Pork Belly with Swiss Chard and Raisin Sauce

Serves
12 to 14

Prep
45 minutes

Total
4 hours, plus curing and pickling

3 bunches Swiss chard, each about
    ¾ pound, leaves cut off stems
Pickling Liquid (see page 270)
4 cups kosher salt, plus more
    for seasoning
2 cups sugar
1 cup sweet paprika (not smoked)
½ whole boneless skin-on pork belly
    (7–8 pounds)
1 cup golden raisins
1 tablespoon lemon juice
2 tablespoons extra-virgin olive oil
2 garlic cloves, thinly sliced
1 tablespoon sherry vinegar

You'll get "oohs" and "aahs" for both the presentation and succulent flavor of this rolled pork belly roast. The skin on the outside crisps into a *chicharrón* crunch that conceals an interior of juicy marbled meat. We temper the delicate richness of it all with pickled chard stems, lemony raisin sauce, and wilted greens. Get it all in one perfect bite—heaven.

Cut the Swiss chard stems crosswise into ¼-inch-thick slices. Place in a jar or other airtight container. Bring the pickling liquid to a boil. Pour over the stems and seal the jar. Refrigerate overnight. Slice the Swiss chard leaves and refrigerate them separately as well.

Mix the salt, sugar, and paprika in a small bowl to make a cure. Sprinkle half in the bottom of a container that will fit the pork belly snugly. Place the meat on top, then cover with the remaining cure mixture. Cover and refrigerate for 4 hours.

Preheat the oven to 325°F.

Rinse the cure off the pork and pat the pork dry. Use a sharp knife to score the meat side (i.e. not the fat side) of the pork with lines ½-inch deep and 2 inches apart going the long way on the belly.

With a long edge of the belly facing you, roll the meat up tightly. Tie the roll with kitchen twine every ½ inch. Place on a wire rack fitted into a half sheet pan.

Bake until the fat renders and the skin is brown, about 2½ hours, or until the internal temperature reaches 145°F.

Raise the oven temperature to 500°F. Roast until the skin is dark brown, dry, and crisp, about 30 minutes, checking at 15-minute intervals. Remove from the oven and let rest for at least 20 minutes.

While the pork rests, make the sauce and greens. Bring 1 cup water to the boil in a small saucepan. Put the raisins in a blender and pour the boiling water over them. Purée until very smooth. Add the lemon juice and purée again. Season to taste with salt.

Combine the oil and garlic in a large skillet. Cook over high heat, stirring, until the garlic is fragrant and golden, about 1 minute. Add the Swiss chard leaves and season with salt. Cook, stirring, until wilted, about 2 minutes. Add the sherry vinegar and mix well, then remove from the heat.

Snip the kitchen twine off the pork and discard. Cut the pork into 1-inch chunks and divide among serving plates. Drain the Swiss chard stems. Serve the pork with the raisin sauce, pickled Swiss chard stems, and wilted Swiss chard greens.

CARRILLERAS DE CERDO

Braised Pork Cheeks

Serves
4 to 6

Prep
20 minutes

Total
3 hours

1 pound pork cheeks, fat trimmed
1 small onion, quartered
1 large carrot, cut into 4 pieces
1 large celery stalk, cut into 4 pieces
2 unpeeled garlic cloves
½ cup dry white wine
½ savoy cabbage
5 ounces chanterelle mushrooms, cleaned
3 sprigs of tarragon
2 tablespoons wholegrain mustard
kosher salt and freshly ground black pepper

We love serving big platters for parties to share. When family and friends are all scooping out of a communal dish, they lean in a little more, share more openly, laugh louder, and have more fun. This stew is a favorite for just that reason. The pork cheeks braise to a melt-in-your-mouth silkiness alongside cabbage and chanterelles that wilt to just-tender in the mustard wine sauce. It's the perfect hearty dish to get people talking at winter holiday gatherings.

Preheat the oven to 375°F.

Season the pork generously with salt and pepper. Put the pork cheeks, onion, carrot, celery, garlic, wine, and 3 cups water in a wide, shallow pot. Bring to a boil over high heat. Cover, transfer to the oven, and bake for 2 hours.

When the cheeks are almost done, heat a grill to high or turn a burner on a gas range to high. Put the cabbage on a rack over the flame and cook, turning, until nicely charred, about 5 minutes. Cut the cabbage in half.

Remove the pot from the oven. Transfer the cheeks to a dish. Strain the pan juices through a fine-mesh sieve; discard the solids. Return the cheeks and strained sauce to the pot. Add the cabbage, chanterelles, and tarragon. Bring to a simmer and simmer for 5 minutes. Season to taste with salt and pepper.

Top with the mustard and serve immediately.

LOMO DE CORDERO

Lamb Loin Roast with Spring Vegetables and Mint

Serves
4 to 6

Prep
45 minutes

Total
2¾ hours, plus overnight marinating

1½ cups shucked fava beans (or use snow peas, English [garden] peas, or green beans)

4 tablespoons extra-virgin olive oil

1 whole lamb loin, excess fat and bone removed (2 pounds)

4 tablespoons unsalted butter

4 garlic cloves, crushed

1 sprig of rosemary

1 sprig of thyme

8 scallions, trimmed

1 bunch of asparagus, trimmed and cut into 3-inch lengths

1 lemon, zest and juice

1 tablespoon fresh mint leaves, plus more for garnish

1 ounce spreadable sheep's milk cheese, crumbled

kosher salt and freshly ground black pepper

Two Catalan classics—roasted lamb and braised fava beans—come together in this spring feast. We've taken a fresh approach to the traditional pairing, combining French technique with New York farm-to-table sensibilities. Garlic-herb butter rolled into a caramelized lamb roast infuses the meat with flavor from the inside out, while asparagus and favas take a quick turn in hot skillet to stay fresh and crisp.

Bring a small saucepan of water to a boil. Fill a medium bowl with ice and water. Add the fava beans to the boiling water and cook until bright green, about 30 seconds. Drain and immediately transfer to the ice water. When cool, drain again, peel off the skins and discard.

Heat 2 tablespoons oil in a large skillet over medium-high heat. Season the lamb with salt and pepper and put skin-side down in the skillet. Sear until the skin is deeply caramelized, about 5 minutes. Turn the lamb over and cook for 3–4 minutes more. Add the butter, garlic, rosemary, and thyme. Use a spoon to continually baste the lamb with the butter mixture for 4 minutes. Transfer the lamb to a rack and let rest for 10 minutes.

Heat a grill to high, or turn a burner on a gas range to high. Put the scallions on a rack over the flame and cook, turning, until nicely charred, about 2 minutes.

Heat the remaining 2 tablespoons oil in a large, deep skillet over high heat. Add the asparagus, season with salt, and cook, stirring, until bright green and crisp-tender, about 3 minutes. Add the fava beans, stir well, and remove from the heat. Season to taste with salt and pepper, then toss with ½ teaspoon lemon juice, charred scallions, and mint leaves.

After the lamb has rested, cut into slices and divide among serving plates, along with the vegetables. Scatter the cheese on top and garnish with mint leaves. Sprinkle the lemon zest on top and serve immediately.

Chef's tip: To trim asparagus—removing the lower, fibrous part of the stalk—hold the stalk near the base with one hand, then use the other hand to bend the stalk over; it will snap naturally about 3 inches above the base, which can then be discarded.

CARNE A LA PLANCHA

Seared Hanger Steak with "Mojo Verde"

Serves
1 or 2

Prep
45 minutes

Total
1 hour

extra-virgin olive oil
1 (8-ounce) hanger steak
4 garlic cloves, crushed
2 sprigs of rosemary
2 sprigs of thyme
4 fingerling potatoes
10 Padrón or shishito peppers
freshly ground black pepper
½ cup Mojo Verde (recipe follows),
    for serving
kosher salt and freshly ground
    black pepper

Spain's Canary Islands sit just west of Africa in the path of the heavy trade winds that shape Morocco's western Sahara. The proximity of North Africa shows in the cuisine of the volcanic islands where local marinades, "mojos," laced with heady spices, flavor meats and stews. The garlicky green version we use here can bring any meat dish to life but goes particularly well with a classic combination of seared steak, potatoes, and peppers (we, of course, use shishitos for an extra bite).

Rub a thin coating of oil all over the steak and then rub with half of the crushed garlic and 1 sprig each of rosemary and thyme. Cover and let stand for 30 minutes at room temperature or refrigerate overnight. If chilled, let stand at room temperature for 30 minutes before cooking.

Preheat the oven to 500°F.

Place the potatoes, remaining garlic, rosemary, and thyme in a small saucepan. Add enough cold water to cover by 1 inch and generously salt the water. Bring to a boil over high heat. Cover, reduce the heat to medium, and simmer until a cake tester or knife pierces a potato easily. Drain well; discard the garlic and herbs. When cool enough to handle, halve each potato lengthwise.

Scrape the garlic and herbs off the steak and discard. Generously season the steak all over with salt. Let stand for 10 minutes.

Heat a large, heavy ovenproof skillet over high heat. Add the steak and cook until well seared, 3–4 minutes per side. Transfer to the oven and roast for 5 minutes for medium-rare. Remove from the oven, transfer to a cutting board, and let rest for 5 minutes.

Meanwhile, heat a large nonstick skillet over high heat. Coat with oil, then add the potatoes in a single layer cut sides down. Cook, shaking the pan occasionally, until the bottoms are lightly browned, about 3 minutes. Scatter the peppers around the potatoes. Generously drizzle the peppers with oil and season with salt. Cook for 2 minutes, carefully but thoroughly toss everything in the pan, and cook for 2 minutes more. The potatoes should be dark brown and the peppers should be blistered and soft. Transfer to paper towels to drain.

Generously season the steak with pepper. Cut into slices and serve with the potatoes, peppers, and mojo verde.

Chef's tips: Hanger steak is an especially juicy cut, but you can also make this with skirt steak if you like.
    Whichever cut you use, you can grill the meat instead of searing and roasting it. Cook the steak on a charcoal or gas grill over medium-high heat for about 6 minutes a side, then let it rest for 5 minutes.

Mojo Verde

Makes about 1⅓ cups
Prep 10 minutes
Total 10 minutes

2 cups cilantro with tender stems
¾ cup flat-leaf parsley leaves
1 garlic clove, peeled and trimmed
½ cubanelle pepper, seeded
   and chopped
½ teaspoon ground cumin
1 cup extra-virgin olive oil
2 tablespoons sherry vinegar
kosher salt

Combine the cilantro, parsley, garlic, pepper, and cumin in a food processor. Pulse, scraping the bowl occasionally, until everything is chopped.

With the machine running, add the oil in a steady stream, then add the vinegar. You want the mixture to be coarse without any large chunks. Pulse more if needed. Season to taste with salt.

Carne a la Plancha (page 206)

CHULETÓN CON ENSALADA DE PATATAS

Grilled Ribeye and Potato Salad

Serves
4 to 6

Prep
45 minutes

Total
1 hour

2 (1½-inch-thick) bone-in prime
ribeye steaks (about 3 pounds total),
preferably dry-aged
Potato Salad (recipe follows)
Spiced Butter (see page 272)
kosher salt and freshly ground
black pepper

Our Spiced Butter (see page 272) drizzled over this steak is outstanding. Clarified, so it's pure savory fat without the sweet cream of dairy, the hot butter sizzles the just-right balance of sweet paprika to hot smoky pimentón. It's a super-easy five-ingredient finish that takes the Basque classic of grilled ribeye over the top. To turn this meaty main into a one-dish meal, we serve it alongside a potato salad freshened up with tender green beans and crunchy red onion and celery.

Allow the steaks to come to room temperature before grilling.

When ready to grill, prepare a charcoal grill with high heat. While the grill heats, season the steaks with salt and pepper and let stand for another 15 minutes.

Grill the steaks until a nice crust forms, 4–5 minutes per side for medium-rare. Let rest on a cutting board for 5–10 minutes.

Cut the steaks across the grain and drizzle with the spiced butter. Serve immediately with the potato salad.

Potato Salad

16 fingerling potatoes
1 sprig of rosemary
1 sprig of thyme
1 garlic clove, peeled
1 cup trimmed green beans
2 celery stalks, thinly sliced,
leaves reserved
¼ red onion, very thinly sliced
3 tablespoons Vinagreta de Jerez
(see page 270)
kosher salt and freshly ground
black pepper

Put the potatoes, rosemary, thyme, garlic, and a generous pinch of salt in a large saucepan of cold water. Bring to a boil over high heat, then reduce the heat to medium and leave the potatoes to boil until they are tender enough for a thin-bladed paring knife to slide through easily, about 20 minutes.

Drain the potatoes and cool. When cool enough to handle, peel the potatoes and cut them into chunks.

Bring a small saucepan of water to a boil. Fill a medium bowl with ice and water. Add the green beans to the boiling water and cook until bright green and crisp-tender, about 3 minutes. Drain and immediately transfer to the ice water. When cool, drain again. Cut in half crosswise.

Combine the potatoes, green beans, celery stalks and leaves, and onion in a large bowl. Season with salt and pepper and toss. Drizzle the vinaigrette on top and toss well.

RABO DE BUEY CON ALBARICOQUES

Braised Oxtails with Apricots

Serves
4 to 6

Prep
45 minutes

Total
3¼–3¾ hours

The Moorish influences in the stunning Andalusían city of Cordoba extend beyond the ornate architecture to the cuisine. Beef reigns here. Cattle are raised on ranches in the surrounding countryside. Inspired by Cordoba's signature braised oxtail and the common use of apricots in Moorish cooking, we created this unctuous stew that combines the two. We braise the oxtails in red wine, tomatoes, and apricots until they collapse at the touch of a fork. The rich red wine and apricot gravy imparts a sweet, fruity tang to the tender meat.

1 cup extra-virgin olive oil

3½ pounds oxtail, each piece cut 2–3 inches thick

½ large white Spanish onion, finely diced

½ head garlic, sliced crosswise through the "equator"

1 celery stalk, leaves removed, sliced

1 carrot, peeled and diced

1 small leek, white and pale green parts only, cut lengthwise then thinly sliced

1 sprig of rosemary

2 sprigs of thyme

2 tomatoes, cut into eighths

22 dried apricots, 8 thinly sliced, 14 kept whole

4 cups dry red wine

2 cups Chicken Stock (see page 268)

kosher salt and freshly ground black pepper

Preheat the oven to 350°F.

Heat the oil in a very large, deep skillet or Dutch oven over high heat until very hot. Generously season the oxtail with salt and pepper. Add the oxtail in a single layer, working in batches if necessary. Cook, turning occasionally to sear evenly, until nicely browned all over, about 20–25 minutes. Transfer to a plate.

Remove all but 2 tablespoons oil from the skillet. Reduce the heat to medium and add the onion, garlic, celery, carrot, leek, rosemary, and thyme. Cook, stirring occasionally, until the vegetables take on color, about 6 minutes.

Add the tomatoes and apricots and stir well. Return the oxtail, along with any accumulated juices, to the skillet, tucking the meat into the vegetables. Add the wine, bring to a boil over high heat, and boil until reduced by half, about 6 minutes. Reduce the heat to medium and turn the pieces of oxtail over. Continue simmering for about 10 minutes.

Add the chicken stock, bring to a boil, then cover and transfer to the oven. Bake until the meat is very tender and almost falling off the bone, about 2½–3 hours.

Transfer the oxtail to a serving dish. If the sauce is too thin, bring to a boil over medium heat. Simmer until reduced and thickened. Spoon over the oxtail and serve hot.

BOQUERIA

POLLASTRE A LA CATALANA

Wine-Braised Chicken with Prunes and Cinnamon

Serves
4 to 6

Prep
15 minutes

Total
2¾ hours

Marc met fellow Catalonian chef Alex Gares when the two cooked together at El Bulli, and they've remained close friends across continents and time. When Marc was creating this classic chicken braise for the book, Alex happened to be staying with him on a New York City vacation and helped with the recipe development. At every step of the process, they argued about the "right" way to do it, each drawing from memories of their grandmothers' versions. They debated how long to brown the chicken, how to cut the onions, whether to leave the garlic peels on, how many prunes to add and at what stage, ditto the wine and cinnamon.

That spirit lies at the heart of Spain's food culture: every dish is worth a fight. Even after years of professional training, the two highly accomplished chefs hold views on how a classic should be done based on their childhood memories. The beauty of this passion is the open give-and-take in the kitchen. Marc let Alex simmer the chicken longer than he would have; Alex conceded to Marc's adding more prunes than he prefers.

The result is a dish even better than the memories. Super simple and comforting, the prunes and caramelized onions melt into the cinnamon-laced wine sauce, perfect for soaking into good bread. And the garlic? The creamy-as-butter cloves end up soft enough to smear onto bread and all over the chicken too.

---

1 whole (3-pound) chicken, cut into
   8 pieces
5 tablespoons extra-virgin olive oil
2 large white Spanish onions, quartered
   and cut into ½-inch slices
10 large garlic cloves with skins left on
1¼ cups pitted prunes
1½ cups dry white wine
2 cinnamon sticks
kosher salt and freshly ground
   black pepper

Generously season the chicken with salt and pepper. Heat the oil in a large, deep skillet over medium-high heat. Add the chicken, skin side down, in a single layer. Cook until the skin is nicely browned and crisp, about 12 minutes. Flip all the pieces and cook until browned, about 7 minutes. Transfer the chicken to a plate.

Add the onions and garlic to the hot pan and season with salt. Reduce the heat to medium and cook, stirring occasionally, until the onions are deeply caramelized and brown, about 20 minutes. Add the prunes, wine, and cinnamon. Bring to a boil, then return the chicken to the pan, skin side up, along with any accumulated juices. Add 1 cup water.

Bring the mixture to a simmer, then reduce the heat to low, cover, and cook until the chicken is very tender, turning the pieces occasionally, about 50 minutes. The meat should be falling off the bone. Let rest in the pan, covered, for at least 20 minutes.

This dish tastes best if made a day ahead and chilled overnight, then reheated.

CONEJO EN SALMOREJO

Marinated and Confited Rabbit

Serves
4 to 6

Prep
45 minutes

Total
2 hours plus marinating

Stop! Don't turn the page. For many American home cooks, rabbit may be intimidating to source and prepare. But the reward far outweighs the risk, especially with this succulent preparation, a regional specialty that Marc learned to cook while working for a summer in the Canary Islands.

A garlicky-spiced oil marinates the meat and simmers it to succulence, then turns into the finishing sauce, too. Gizzards, seared until just caramelized then blended into the same marinade, give the sauce a silky richness. Combined with the tender confited meat, the sauce delivers a decadence that will make your heart hop for rabbit.

---

12 dried bay leaves

2 tablespoons dried oregano

1 tablespoon dried thyme

1 tablespoon cumin seeds

2 tablespoons sweet pimentón

4 garlic cloves, peeled

2 guindilla peppers or chiles de árbol

2 tablespoons dry white wine

2 tablespoons white wine vinegar

3⅓ cups extra-virgin olive oil, plus
   more as needed

1 large rabbit (3 ½ pounds), cut in
   8 pieces, plus its kidneys, liver,
   and gizzards

kosher salt

To make the marinade: pulse the bay leaves, oregano, thyme, and cumin in a spice grinder (or grind with a mortar and pestle) until finely ground. Transfer to a blender or food processor and add the pimentón, garlic, guindillas, and 1 teaspoon salt. Pulse, scraping the bowl occasionally, until the mixture is blended. Add the wine and vinegar and pulse until the mixture forms a paste. With the machine running, add 1 cup oil in a steady stream.

Place the rabbit meat, excluding the offal, in an airtight container and add the marinade. Turn until well coated. Cover and refrigerate for 12 hours.

Heat 3 tablespoons oil in a very large skillet over high heat. Generously season the rabbit kidneys, liver, and gizzards with salt. Add to the hot oil and sear, turning to brown evenly, until nearly cooked through, about 4 minutes. They should still be a little raw inside. Remove from the heat and transfer to a mortar. Pound until smashed (you may need to do this in batches). Or pulse in a food processor until coarsely chopped. Reserve the skillet, without washing, for use later.

Lift the rabbit pieces out of the marinade. Pour the oil from the marinade into the mortar, or food processor, with the smashed offal and stir until the mixture forms a smooth paste. Add more olive oil if needed to form the paste.

Heat 2 tablespoons oil in a large skillet over high heat. Season the rabbit pieces with salt and add to the skillet in a single layer. Work in batches if necessary to avoid overcrowding the pan. Cook until the undersides are browned, about 4 minutes. Flip and cook for 1 minute more. Transfer the rabbit to a plate and pour any accumulated pan juices into the mortar, or food processor.

Return the rabbit to the skillet and add the remaining 2 cups oil. It should cover almost all of the meat. Add more if needed. Bring to a simmer over medium heat, then reduce the heat to low to simmer, turning the meat occasionally, until the meat is cooked through and tender, about 20 minutes.

Remove from the heat and stir in the sauce from the mortar, or food processor. Cover and let stand for a few hours. When ready to serve, reheat over medium heat until hot.

DESSERTS

DESSERTS

Our dessert menu celebrates the comforting sweets that cap the daily laid-back Spanish midday meal. Hearty arroz con leche or glossy crema catalana. Fresh cheese with fruits and honey or sticky bread pudding—every home and restaurant has a specialty.

It's while lingering at the table over these sweets that the most important of all Spanish mealtime traditions begins, the "sobremesa" ("over the table"). At this long end-of-the-meal conversation family and friends cover all topics from gossip and politics to life's greatest mysteries.

Sometimes the hardest questions have the simplest answers. "Why are we here?" To eat this incredibly smooth and silky flan, of course.

FRESAS CON MATÓ, MIEL Y NUECES

Strawberries with Ricotta, Honey, and Walnuts

Makes
8

Prep
10 minutes

Total
10 minutes

Honey drizzled over fresh cheese: that's the classic Catalan dessert *mel i mato*. It symbolizes the cuisine's commitment to treating the best products simply to let them shine. To build on that celebration of local ingredients, Marc took inspiration from his time at Barcelona's Windsor Restaurant. Each week, a farmer from nearby Girona brought Marc a few rounds of fresh *el recuit de fonteta* cheese. To highlight the cheese's super fresh creaminess, Marc simply drizzled mounds with honey and scattered berries and nuts on top. You can do the same at home or follow the easy plating instructions below for a dessert elegant enough for a dinner party. Just be sure to start with the best locally produced and grown fresh cheese, honey, and berries.

---

8 walnuts
8 large strawberries
½ cup fresh ricotta
honey, for drizzling
1 orange

Toast the walnuts in a small skillet over medium heat until golden brown and crisp, about 4 minutes. Leave to cool completely.

Using a small paring knife, trim the tops of the strawberries to make a flat space large enough to hold a tablespoonful of the ricotta. Cut a little across the bottoms so that the berries will stand up on the plate. Cut out the cores from the tops. Sit the strawberries on their bottoms on a serving plate. Dollop 1 tablespoon ricotta on top of each berry.

Drizzle honey all over the berries and ricotta, then zest the orange directly on top. Gently press 1 walnut into the ricotta on each berry. Serve immediately.

Chef's tips: You could use the leftover strawberry bits as topping for cereal or vanilla ice cream.

If you're not using fresh ricotta, strain it overnight in a cheesecloth-lined strainer to remove excess liquid.

TORRIJA

French Toast with Yogurt Ice Cream, Berries, and Toffee Sauce

Serves
3 to 6

Prep
30 minutes

Total
1 hour, plus soaking

2 large eggs
1 cup whole milk
1 cup heavy cream
3 (2-inch-thick) slices dense brioche
    or pullman bread, crusts cut off,
    each piece cut in half vertically
2 tablespoons clarified butter
    (see page 272)
8 tablespoons coarse raw sugar
plain store-bought yogurt ice cream,
    for serving
berries, for serving
Toffee Sauce (recipe follows),
    for serving
confectioners' sugar, for
    serving, optional

You will need:
a blowtorch

Toffee Sauce

Makes about 1¼ cups
Prep 10 minutes
Total 20 minutes

⅔ cup sugar
¼ cup water
¾ cup heavy cream
2 tablespoons salted butter, softened
pinch of kosher salt

Torrija is the most sensual version of French toast you can imagine. Milk-soaked bread is coated in egg and fried, then finished with a generous sprinkle of sugar. We've doubled down on the original's richness by sizzling custard-drenched brioche slices in clarified butter and coarse sugar, then caramelizing more sugar on top with a blowtorch. To take it over the top, we drizzle it all with toffee sauce and scoop on some ice cream.

Whisk the eggs in a medium bowl, then whisk in the milk and cream until smooth. Put the bread slices in a container that fits them snugly and pour the egg-milk mixture over the bread to soak evenly. Refrigerate, turning occasionally, until the bread is completely soaked and soft, about 45 minutes–1 hour.

Preheat the oven to 400°F.

Swirl the clarified butter in a large nonstick skillet over medium-high heat. Sprinkle 2 tablespoons raw sugar over the butter to evenly coat the bottom. When the butter is hot but the sugar is still granular, add the soaked bread in a single layer. Cook until nicely browned, about 1 minute per side. Transfer to a nonstick sheet pan, then transfer to the oven. Bake until a cake tester inserted in the center of one comes out hot, about 6 minutes.

Sprinkle the top of each piece with 1 tablespoon raw sugar. Use a blowtorch to caramelize the sugar on top, burning much of it to a dark brown.

Divide the pieces among serving plates and top with the ice cream and berries. Drizzle all over with the toffee sauce and dust with confectioners' sugar, if you like. Serve immediately.

Combine the sugar and water in a medium saucepan. Cook over medium-high heat, swirling the pan occasionally but not stirring, until boiling, about 2 minutes. Reduce the heat to low and continue cooking until the mixture becomes a dark amber caramel, about 5 minutes.

Remove from the heat and very carefully add the cream in a slow, steady stream while whisking continuously. Be careful! The caramel is extremely hot and will bubble up.

Set over low heat and return to a boil. Remove from the heat and carefully whisk in the butter until smooth and shiny, then whisk in the salt. Transfer to a container and let cool to room temperature, about 30 minutes. (To speed this up, place it in the refrigerator.)

The sauce will keep well, refrigerated, for up to 1 week. Bring to room temperature before serving.

TARTA DE CHOCOLATE CON NUECES Y CAFÉ

Chocolate Tart with Walnuts and Coffee Cream

Makes
One 8-inch cake for 10 to 12

Prep
45 minutes

Total
1½ hours, plus cooling

This crustless tart defies logic. It manages to taste as light as a sponge cake and as fudgy as a brownie all at the same time. The magical mixture, laced with toasted walnuts, spotlights the intensity of bittersweet chocolate, as do the chocolate-sherry glaze and coffee whipped cream.

---

9 tablespoons unsalted butter, softened, plus more for the pan
all-purpose flour, for dusting
4½ ounces bittersweet chocolate, preferably 70 percent cocoa solids, chopped
5 large eggs, at room temperature
¾ cup plus 2 tablespoons sugar
⅔ cup cake flour
2 teaspoons baking powder
½ cup roughly chopped walnuts, toasted
Chocolate Pedro Ximénez Glaze (recipe follows)
Coffee Cream (recipe follows), for serving

Preheat the oven to 325°F. Generously butter an 8-inch springform pan. Dust with flour and tap out excess.

Put the chocolate in a large heatproof bowl. Set over a saucepan of simmering water and melt, stirring occasionally, until smooth. Remove from the saucepan. Add the butter, a tablespoon at a time, and stir until very smooth and well mixed. Let cool while you beat the eggs.

Using the whisk attachment in a stand mixer on medium-high speed, beat the eggs until well blended. Add the sugar, a little at a time so it doesn't fly everywhere. Raise the speed to high and beat until the mixture is a pale cream color and has tripled in volume.

Transfer one-third of the beaten eggs to the chocolate mixture and whisk gently until smooth. Add the remaining beaten eggs and very gently fold in with a spatula until incorporated. You don't want to deflate the mixture.

Stir the flour and baking powder together in a small bowl, then sift over the chocolate mixture. Very gently fold in the flour until thoroughly incorporated. Fold in the walnuts until evenly distributed.

Spread the batter in the pan. Tap the pan against the work surface to smooth and flatten the top.

Bake until the top looks dry and cracked and barely springs back when gently pressed with your fingertip, about 35 minutes.

Cool in the pan on a wire rack for 15 minutes, then remove the sides of the pan. Carefully invert the cake onto the rack and remove the bottom of the pan. Cool completely.

Let the chocolate glaze cool until just warm to the touch. Slowly pour over the cake on the rack (on the smooth bottom) in a circular motion to evenly coat the top and let drip down the sides.

When ready to serve, use a warm knife to cut the cake into wedges. Top each wedge with the whipped coffee cream. Serve immediately.

Chocolate Pedro Ximénez Glaze

½ cup Pedro Ximénez sherry
1 tablespoon sugar
5 ounces bittersweet chocolate,
    preferably 70 percent cocoa solids,
    chopped
1 tablespoon extra-virgin olive oil

Bring the Pedro Ximénez and sugar to a boil in a small saucepan. Boil until reduced to 2 tablespoons, about 20 minutes.

Meanwhile, melt the chocolate in a heatproof bowl set over a saucepan of simmering water, stirring until smooth. Stir in the sherry reduction and the oil until smooth.

Coffee Cream

1 cup heavy cream
1 tablespoon sugar
1 tablespoon instant coffee, preferably
    Classic Nescafé

Combine the cream and sugar in a medium saucepan. Bring to a boil over medium heat, then remove from the heat. Whisk in the coffee until it is dissolved and the cream is evenly tan in color. Refrigerate until very cold, preferably overnight.

Whisk the cold cream by hand until very soft peaks form. Use immediately.

Tarta de Chocolate con Nueces y Café (page 226)

TARTA DE MANZANA
Apple Tart

Makes
one 9-inch tart

Prep
35 minutes

Total
2 hours, plus cooling

3 Golden Delicious apples
2 tablespoons unsalted butter
good pinch saffron threads
3 tablespoons sugar, plus more
    for serving
1 sheet (about 250 grams) frozen
    puff pastry, thawed

You will need:
a blowtorch

One of Marc's lasting memories of working with famed chef Alain Passard is rolling perfect puff pastry and transforming it into fruit tarts. He does the same now, topping pastry with peaches and lavender cream in the summer and saffron-scented apples all fall and winter. At home, you can use high-quality, store-bought, all-butter puff pastry instead of making your own and still end up with a fantastic dessert because the apple filling is so mouthwatering.

Peel, quarter, core, and thinly slice two of the apples. Put them in a medium saucepan, along with the butter, saffron, 1 tablespoon sugar, and 3 tablespoons water. Cover and cook over medium heat, stirring occasionally, until the mixture is dry, about 18 minutes. Blend on high speed until very smooth. Cool completely.

Preheat the oven to 425°F.

On a lightly floured surface, roll the pastry into a 10-inch square. Place a 9½-inch-diameter dinner plate on the pastry and cut around it. (Discard the scraps or reserve for another use.) Place the pastry circle on a parchment-paper-lined baking sheet.

Using an apple corer, remove the core from the remaining apple, then cut each half into scant $\frac{1}{16}$-inch-thick slices. If you have a mandoline, use it for this.

Spread the cooled apple purée over the pastry, leaving a ½-inch rim. Fan the sliced apple over the purée in slightly overlapping circles. Sprinkle the remaining 2 tablespoons sugar over the sliced apple.

Bake until the pastry is golden brown and the apples on top are tender and caramelized, about 45 minutes.

Cool slightly, then sprinkle the apples with more sugar to coat lightly. Use a blowtorch to caramelize the sugar on top. Serve warm.

TURRÓN

Hazelnut Cake with Caramelized Hazelnuts

Serves
4

Prep
1 hour

Total
1½ hours, plus cooling

4 tablespoons unsalted butter,
    softened, plus more for the pan
all-purpose flour, for dusting
3½ ounces hazelnut praline
3 large eggs
¾ cup confectioners' sugar, sifted
1¼ cups almond flour
Vanilla Whipped Cream (recipe
    follows), for serving
Caramelized Hazelnuts (recipe
    follows), for serving
honey, for drizzling
store-bought dulce de leche ice cream,
    for serving
Maldon sea salt flakes, for sprinkling

Spain's iconic nut-studded honey nougat is a Christmas treat, but you'll want to make this dessert all year. We've transformed the candy's flavors into a tender, buttery, almond-hazelnut cake topped with candied hazelnuts and a drizzle of honey. The dual creaminess of dulce de leche ice cream and freshly whipped vanilla cream and a final sprinkle of sea salt balance the sweetness perfectly.

Preheat the oven to 350°F. Generously butter an 8-inch-diameter, 2-inch-deep cake pan. Dust with flour and tap out excess.

Combine the butter and hazelnut praline in a large heatproof bowl. Set over a saucepan of simmering water and melt the butter. Remove the bowl from the saucepan and whisk until as smooth as possible. Let cool to room temperature.

Beat the eggs with the whisk attachment of an electric stand mixer on medium-high speed until well blended. Add the confectioners' sugar, a little at a time so it doesn't fly everywhere. Raise the speed to high and beat until the mixture is a pale cream color and has tripled in volume, about 10 minutes.

Transfer one-third of the beaten eggs to the butter mixture and whisk gently until smooth. Add the remaining beaten eggs and very gently fold in with a spatula until incorporated. You don't want to deflate the mixture. Very gently fold in the almond flour until thoroughly incorporated.

Pour the batter into the prepared pan. Gently tap the pan against a work surface to smooth and flatten the top.

Bake until a cake tester inserted in the center comes out clean, about 40 minutes.

Cool in the pan on a wire rack. Unmold when warm or at room temperature.

To plate, cut the cake in quarters and put one quarter on each serving plate. Plop a scoop of whipped cream on each piece. Add the caramelized hazelnuts, then drizzle the honey on top and lightly sprinkle with the sea salt flakes. Serve immediately with a scoop of the ice cream on the side.

Chef's tips: If you want to make this dessert gluten-free, use nonstick cooking spray to coat the cake pan instead of butter and flour.
    You can buy hazelnut praline online or in specialty shops.

Vanilla Whipped Cream

Makes 2 cups

1 cup heavy whipping cream
½ vanilla bean, split lengthwise, seeds scraped and reserved
1 tablespoon sugar

Combine the cream, vanilla seeds and pod, and sugar in a medium saucepan. Bring to a boil over medium heat, then remove from the heat. Strain through a fine-mesh sieve into a large bowl. Refrigerate until very cold, preferably overnight.

Whisk the cold cream by hand until very soft peaks form. Use immediately.

Caramelized Hazelnuts

Makes 1 cup

¼ cup sugar
1 cup hazelnuts, toasted and skinned
1 tablespoon clarified butter (see page 272)

Combine the sugar and ¼ cup water in a large, deep saucepan. Cook without stirring on high heat until the mixture bubbles like lava. Add the hazelnuts and stir well, then remove from the heat. Keep stirring until the sugar caramelizes into a powdery coating on the nuts. Continue stirring while shaking the pan until the nuts are evenly coated.

Using a slotted spoon, transfer the nuts to another saucepan, leaving the sugar in the first saucepan. Add the clarified butter to the nuts and set over low heat.

Cook, stirring the nuts and shaking the pan, until the sugar melts again and the nuts are caramelized. Using a spoon, immediately transfer them to a sheet of parchment paper, leaving any excess butter in the pan.

Use two spoons to quickly and carefully separate the nuts on the parchment paper. Be careful: they're very hot. Cool completely on the parchment, then break apart any nuts that are still stuck together. Chop the nuts coarsely.

Turrón (page 232)

ARROZ CON LECHE

Rice Pudding with Lemon Zest Purée

Serves
4

Prep
45 minutes

Total
1 hour, plus 2 hours' chilling

Our take on this classic Spanish dessert is deliciously creamy. We stir it risotto-style, adding the milk little by little so the bomba rice grains explode and release their sweet starch into the mix. To balance that lusciousness, we swap the standard cinnamon garnish for tangy lemon zest purée and lime zest. Both bring a tart citrus kick that makes the milky pudding that much more delicious.

---

4 cups whole milk
1 cup heavy cream
1 vanilla bean, split lengthwise, seeds scraped
¼ cup bomba rice
½ cup sugar
3 tablespoons unsalted butter, at room temperature
1 teaspoon fresh lime zest
Lemon Zest Purée (recipe follows), to serve

Combine the milk and cream in a large saucepan. Add the vanilla seeds and pod to the saucepan. Bring to a boil over medium heat, whisking occasionally to distribute the seeds evenly. Remove from the heat.

Pour ½ cup of the hot milk mixture through a fine-mesh sieve into another saucepan. Stir in the rice. Cook over medium heat, stirring, until the milk is reduced, about 4 minutes. Repeat, adding ½ cup milk at a time, until all the milk has been added. It will take about 4 minutes after each addition for the milk to reduce before the next can be added. Be sure to stir continuously to prevent the bottom from scorching and to help the rice release its starches.

After all the milk has been added, reduce the heat to low and cook, stirring occasionally, until the rice grains have burst and the mixture is the consistency of thick pancake batter, about 15 minutes. Remove from the heat and add the sugar and butter. Mix until fully incorporated.

Transfer to a bowl, press plastic wrap directly against the surface of the pudding, and refrigerate until cold.

When ready to serve, stir to loosen and divide among serving bowls. Zest the lime directly on top, then spoon on the lemon zest purée.

Lemon Zest Purée

Makes about ½ cup

5 lemons
2 tablespoons sugar
1 tablespoon unsalted butter, at room temperature

Remove the zest from the lemons in long strips using a vegetable peeler; reserve the lemons. Place the zest in a small saucepan and add enough cold water to cover. Bring to a boil over high heat, then drain well. Repeat 3 times, using fresh cold water each time. The zest should be very soft after the final boiling and draining.

Place the sugar in a blender. Squeeze 5 tablespoons juice from the reserved lemons and add to the sugar, along with 2 teaspoons water. Purée until well mixed. Add the butter and lemon zest. Purée until extremely smooth, scraping the container occasionally.

Transfer to a bowl, press plastic wrap directly against the surface to prevent a skin from forming, and refrigerate until cold.

BUDÍN DE LA ABUELA
Caramel Bread Pudding

Makes
one 9- by 5-inch loaf

Prep
30 minutes

Total
1 hour, plus cooling (8 hours or
overnight)

softened butter or cooking oil,
   for greasing
1¼ cups sugar
1½ cups whole milk
½ vanilla bean, split lengthwise,
   seeds scraped
3 large eggs
13 ounces (about 5–6 cups) pastries,
   preferably a mix of croissants,
   almond croissants, chocolate
   croissants, cinnamon rolls,
   and brioche

Imagine the amber caramel of flan flooding a traditional bread pudding. Yes, it's that good. The fusion of those two desserts comes courtesy of Marc's grandmother. Every day, she set her bread pudding on the restaurant's counter and cut portions for customers who wanted a hunk. And everyone did. It was her way of using up old pastries and making her diners happy in the process. Keeping the thrifty and comforting spirit of the original, Marc uses day-old pastries to turn out a pudding with complex layers of textures and sweetness.

Preheat the oven to 400°F and grease a 9 x 5 x 4-inch loaf pan with softened butter/cooking oil.

Combine 1 cup sugar with ⅓ cup of water in a large saucepan. Cook over medium heat, swirling the pan occasionally but not stirring, until boiling, about 4 minutes. Reduce the heat to low and continue cooking until the mixture becomes a dark amber caramel, about 6 minutes. Add 2 tablespoons water and mix in well; this will soften the caramel a little.

Very carefully pour the hot caramel into the greased loaf pan. (Reserve the saucepan for use later.) Swirl it to completely coat the bottom and 2 inches up the sides of the pan.

Combine the milk and vanilla seeds and half pod in the saucepan used for the caramel. Bring to a simmer over medium heat, about 5 minutes. Mix well to disperse the vanilla seeds, then remove from the heat and let steep for at least 5 minutes. Strain through a fine-mesh sieve into a large (minimum 4 cups) measuring cup.

Whisk the eggs with the remaining ¼ cup sugar in a large bowl until blended. Add the milk mixture in a steady stream while whisking until smooth.

Tear all of the pastries into 2- to 3-inch pieces, then pack them into the loaf pan. Carefully pour the egg-milk mixture over the pastries; press down the pastries to make sure they're all fully immersed in the liquid.

Bake in the center of the oven until golden brown and cooked through, about 45 minutes. Cool in the pan on a wire rack overnight. Center a serving plate over the pan and carefully flip both together. Lift off the loaf pan, cut into slices, and serve.

CREMA CATALANA

Caramelized Cinnamon-Citrus Custard

Makes
4

Prep
35 minutes

Total
45 minutes plus chilling

The first thing that hits you when you step into Catalonia's oldest restaurants is a whiff of fireplace meets caramel. The scent is something like a s'more but with the depth of age. What you're smelling is the crackling caramelized top of crema catalana, the region's most iconic dessert. These old-school spots use a branding iron heated in a wood fire to burn the sugar, so you get smokiness with each spoonful. Underneath that shell is a cinnamon-vanilla custard, thick and rich with a henhouse of egg yolks. We add citrus zest for a touch of brightness.

You can get a hint of that live fire aroma at home simply by blowtorching the sugar on top; just be sure to let it get dark brown. That bitter edge keeps the sweet custard in check.

¾ cup sugar, plus more for serving
¼ cup cornstarch
6 large egg yolks
4 cups milk
1 vanilla bean, split lengthwise, seeds scraped
1 cinnamon stick
1 strip of lemon zest, removed with a vegetable peeler
1 strip of orange zest, removed with a vegetable peeler

You will need:
a blowtorch

Fill the bottom of a double boiler with water and bring to a simmer. In the top pan (working on the countertop) whisk together the sugar and cornstarch until combined. Add the egg yolks and ¼ cup milk. Whisk the mixture well. (If you don't have a double boiler you can use a large, deep skillet for the water and a saucepan that will fit inside it for the egg yolk mixture.)

Combine the remaining 3¾ cups milk with the vanilla pod and seeds, cinnamon stick, and lemon and orange zest in a saucepan. Bring to a simmer over medium heat, stirring occasionally. Remove from the heat. Strain through a fine-mesh sieve into a large measuring cup.

Whisk the egg yolk mixture while adding the milk mixture in a slow, steady stream. Once all of the milk is incorporated, set the pan over the simmering water. Cook, whisking continuously, until the mixture is a thick custard sauce.

Divide the mixture among four 5½-inch-diameter, 1-inch-deep crema catalana (or crème brûlée) dishes. The dishes should be filled to the top. Tap the dishes against the countertop to flatten the tops. Transfer to the refrigerator and chill until cold, 4 hours or overnight.

When ready to serve, sprinkle the tops of the cremas evenly with sugar. Use a blowtorch to caramelize the sugar on the tops to a dark brown. Serve immediately.

FLAN CASERO

Vanilla-Coffee Custard with Caramel

Serves
12

Prep
about 20 minutes

Total
1½ hours, plus cooling

3 cups sugar
3½ cups whole milk
½ cup heavy cream
8 coffee beans
1 vanilla bean, split lengthwise,
    seeds scraped
8 large eggs, at room temperature

You will need:
a fluted baking pan with a capacity
    of 10 cups

Unmolding a flan and seeing the caramel run down the sides of a wobbly golden custard is one of baking's most satisfying experiences; second only to eating it. We've infused the creamy egg blend with both vanilla and coffee for their deep aromas. Though the flavors are complex, the execution is easy. Since flan needs to be chilled for a while before serving, it's the ideal make-ahead party dessert.

Preheat the oven to 350°F with a rack in the center.

Combine 2 cups sugar with ½ cup water in a large saucepan. Cook over medium heat, swirling the pan occasionally but not stirring, until boiling, about 6 minutes. Reduce the heat to low and continue cooking until the mixture becomes a dark amber caramel, about 10 minutes, and reaches a temperature of about 335–345°F on a candy thermometer.

While the caramel is cooking, combine the milk, cream, coffee beans, and vanilla seeds and pod in another large saucepan. Bring to a simmer over medium heat, about 6 minutes. Mix well to disperse the vanilla seeds, then remove from the heat and let steep for at least 5 minutes. Strain through a fine-mesh sieve into a large pitcher.

As soon as the caramel reaches the desired color, immediately and very carefully pour it into the fluted pan. If the bottom of the pan is not evenly covered, swirl to move the caramel over the surface. Place the pan in a roasting pan.

Whisk the eggs with the remaining 1 cup sugar in a large bowl until blended. Continue whisking, while adding the milk mixture in a steady stream, until the mixture is smooth. Ladle the mixture into the fluted pan; it should come to within ⅛-inch of the rim.

Bring a kettle of water to a boil. Carefully pour the hot water into the roasting pan, without splattering into the flan, until the water comes halfway up the side of the fluted pan. Very carefully transfer the roasting pan to the oven. Bake until a thin-bladed knife comes out clean when inserted into the center of the flan, about 1 hour. Be sure to avoid overcooking; the flan should jiggle slightly.

Carefully remove the fluted pan from the water and let cool to room temperature on a cooling rack. Transfer to the refrigerator and chill overnight until cold.

When ready to serve, run a thin-bladed paring knife around the edge of the flan. Center a serving plate over the pan and flip the plate and pan together. Lift off the pan, letting all the caramel drip onto the plate.

CHURROS

Traditional Spanish Doughnuts

Serves
4

Prep
30 minutes

Total
40 minutes

In Spain, revelers often end a long night of partying with a visit to a churro shop where they order the irresistible golden-fried pastries and dunk them in a traditional thick hot chocolate. At Boqueria, churros also make for the perfect sweet ending to a great night. We build ice cream sundaes around them, use them as cookies for gooey s'mores, and stuff them with Nutella and dulce de leche. But no version is more popular than the most traditional featured here. These churros fry to a golden crisp with a soft, steamy center, their thin crevices engineered to pick up just the right amount of the rich, dark chocolate.

---

1 cup milk
1¼ cups water
2 cups flour
1 quart blended canola-olive oil, for deep frying
Sugar and Cinnamon Mix (recipe follows)
Chocolate Sauce (recipe follows)
kosher salt

In a saucepan, combine the milk, water, and salt and bring to boil. Take off the heat and add the flour and mix until no lumps remain, about 3 minutes.

Transfer the dough to the bowl of a stand mixer fitted with the paddle attachment. Beat on medium speed, about 3 minutes.

Meanwhile, in a large saucepan heat the canola-olive oil blend to 350°F.

When the dough is ready, transfer it to a double pastry bag or a churro making tool. Squeeze approximately 4 inches of churro dough from the pastry bag or churro tool directly into the hot oil. Repeat with as many churros as you can fit in the pan without over-crowding (you can do this in batches if necessary). Fry the churros, moving constantly, until golden brown, making sure they are cooked on the inside. This should take about 3–4 minutes per batch.

Once golden, remove the churros from the oil with a slotted spoon and set on paper towels to drain any excess oil. While still hot, roll each churro through the sugar mix and serve with the chocolate sauce for dipping.

Sugar and Cinnamon Mix

1 cup sugar
1 tablespoon cinnamon

Mix the sugar and cinnamon together in a bowl and set aside.

Chocolate Sauce

1 pint milk
¼ cup sugar
1 teaspoon cornstarch
1 cup chocolate, preferably 70 percent cocoa solids, chopped

In a saucepan bring the milk and sugar to boil.

In a separate bowl, mix the cornstarch with 2 tablespoons of the hot milk. Once the mixture is smooth, incorporate into the rest of the boiling milk and take off the heat.

Put the chocolate pieces in another bowl. Add a little of the hot milk and mix with chocolate. Continue adding the milk, little by little, until all of the milk is used and the chocolate is melted. Let cool and set aside until needed.

DRINKS

DRINKS

Tapas were originally created by barkeeps to attract customers. They gave away small, salty snacks to keep patrons on their stools sipping away for a few more rounds. From those humble beginnings, tapas have evolved into the sophisticated dishes you have learned to prepare in this book. One thing, however, has not changed: free-flowing drinks and conversation are as intrinsic to the tapas experience as ever.

In Spain, ice-cold draft beers enjoy top billing at tapas spots everywhere, but regional preferences abound. Andalusíans opt for nutty manzanilla or fino sherry, while Basques prefer txakoli (pronounced "chalk OH lee"), a crisp, effervescent local white wine. Catalans revere vermouth, but Navarros are partial to *potes*, two-sip glasses of red wine, perfect for a one-

tapa pit-stop. New Yorkers? They like to kick things off with a well-crafted cocktail before tucking in.

At Boqueria we honor all these traditions. Our beverage menu winds through all of Spain before jumping across the Pond for a lap around the five New York boroughs, picking up wines, spirits, and regional favorites along the way. There is something for everyone and for every occasion. But sangría, usually reserved in Spain for parties at home, has emerged as our guests' absolute favorite. Pitchers full of seasonal favorites and house classics paint a rainbow across our dining room every day of the week. For most of our guests, their favorite Boqueria experience always begins with the familiar swoosh of liquid and clink of ice as it fills their first glass.

BOQUERIA

Wine

A few years back, we had a chance to visit Mallorca with Miguelangel Cerdá, a winemaker most famous for his cult favorite Ànima Negra. He walked us through the fields surrounding a small vineyard and pointed out the different wild herbs that grew among the gnarled, weathered vines. "They are the most fragrant herbs on the island," he declared, as the wind stirred up his curly hair. Big puffy clouds pushed shadows across the fields, and, from the center of the vineyard, we could see a falcon making lazy circles over the rocky, shrubbed landscape.

Miguelangel pointed to the vines and then to a couple of wind-warped apricot trees at the center of the vineyard. "These are the best grapes on the island, and those are the sweetest apricots. They are also the last of each to ripen. Why do you think?" We looked at each other, anxious to get the answer right. "The elevation?" "The sun exposure?" "Something in the soil?"

He shook his head. "No. Look around again. Have you ever seen a place so beautiful?" We gazed out past an old stone barn and watched the picturesque landscape in its crumbling descent toward the sea. His voice lowered to a whisper. "The fruit ripens last here because it doesn't want to leave this beauty. It hangs on as long as it can. It is the sweetest because life here is so good."

Every time we uncork a bottle of Miguelangel's Ànima Negra, we watch all the beauty of Mallorca spill out into the glasses in front of us. And that magic happens with every wine on our list. They all come from Spain, and each bottle holds a message from its origin. Crisp, white albariño speaks in a sea-salty lilt from Galicia's green coast. A ripe Catalan cariñena tells its story in the stony aromas and rugged tannins it stole from the craggy slate cliffs and toasty afternoons of Priorat.

Spanish tapas taste best with Spanish wine. When choosing a bottle or two for your dinner, there are a few general comparisons with wines from other countries that can make this easier. When it comes to whites, pinot grigio and sauvignon blanc drinkers usually love albariño or verdejo, whereas chardonnay drinkers appreciate white Rioja or garnacha blanca. When looking for a bold red, lovers of cabernet and malbec should choose Priorat or Ribera del Duero, and pinot noir junkies will fall in love with mencia.

The best choice of all? Nothing beats a tapas feast with plenty of sparkling cava and red Rioja; both are versatile and delicious and pair well with almost everything.

SANGRÍA DE SANDÍA

Watermelon Sangría

Serves
8 to 10

Prep
45 minutes

Total
45 minutes, plus infusing and chilling

We threw our tenth anniversary party in the dog days of summer and wanted something special and refreshing to welcome a decade of staff and regulars.

Kieran Chavez, our Beverage Director, worked as a server at our first little outpost right when we opened, so who better to come up with something to celebrate? His watermelon sangría was such a hit at the party we put it on all of our menus. Much like Kieran himself, it's cool and festive, and it packs a punch. Make this refreshing sangría your go-to summer barbeque beverage.

2½ cups watermelon chunks (from a baby watermelon weighing about 14 ounces), plus more if needed, and wedges for serving
1 bottle (750ml) dry white wine, preferably Garnacha Blanca, unoaked Godello, or Viura
8½ fluid ounces good-quality London dry gin, preferably Fords
4½ fluid ounces lemon juice
5 fluid ounces Basil Syrup (recipe follows)
pinch of sea salt

Purée the watermelon chunks in a blender on medium speed until completely juiced. Strain through a fine-mesh sieve into a container, cover, and refrigerate until cold. You should have 1¼ cups juice. If you don't, purée and strain more watermelon chunks.

Mix the watermelon juice, wine, gin, lemon juice, basil syrup, and salt in a large pitcher until the salt has dissolved. Refrigerate if the mixture isn't very cold. Serve on the same day.

When ready to serve, place one watermelon wedge in each serving glass and fill with ice. Stir the sangría well to mix the watermelon juice if it has separated. Divide among the glasses and serve immediately.

Chef's tip: If you wish to prepare the watermelon juice a day ahead, line the strainer with a coffee filter, place the strainer over a bowl, then add the purée; refrigerate overnight. Discard the pulp. The filter paper will prevent the juice from separating and taking on a stale flavor, as it is likely to do if left too long. You may need to use more watermelon chunks in order to get the required amount of juice.

Basil Syrup

½ cup sugar
7 basil leaves with tender stems

Bring ½ cup water to a boil in a small saucepan. Add the sugar, stirring until it dissolves, then remove from the heat and let cool for 5 minutes.

Tear each basil leaf in thirds and add to the syrup with their tender stems. Cover and infuse for 2 hours. Strain through a fine-mesh sieve into a container, cover, and refrigerate until cold.

SANGRÍA DE VINO ROSADO

Rosé Sangría

Makes
4¾ cups

Prep
15 minutes

Total
15 minutes, plus chilling

2¼ cups mixed cut fruit, such as slices of plums, other stone fruit, and halved grapes

1 fluid ounce orange liqueur, such as Triple Sec, for marinating

1 bottle (750ml) dry, pale rosé wine, preferably from Rioja, chilled

4½ fluid ounces silver tequila, preferably Cimarron, chilled

3½ fluid ounces cranberry juice, chilled

2½ fluid ounces pomegranate juice, chilled

2 tablespoons Simple Syrup (see page 261), or to taste, chilled

Pretty in pink, light, and crisp, this rosé potion tiptoes between sweet and tart with both cranberry and pomegranate juices. It may look delicate, but it takes no prisoners. It's our booziest option with a generous dose of tequila. Consider yourself warned.

Put the fruit in an airtight container. Toss with a little orange liqueur to barely coat the fruit. Cover and refrigerate at least a few hours and up to overnight.

Mix the rosé, tequila, cranberry juice, pomegranate juice, and simple syrup in a large pitcher. Taste and add more syrup if desired. Refrigerate if the mixture isn't very cold. You can chill this mixture until you're ready to serve, for up to 3 days.

When ready to serve, drain the fruit and divide among serving glasses. Top with the chilled sangría and serve immediately.

SANGRÍA DE VINO TINTO

Red Sangría

Serves
10 to 12

Prep
30 minutes

Total
30 minutes, plus chilling

Boqueria is all about feeling like a party. And there's no better party drink than sangría. Every night, at every location, we ladle out glass after glass for customers at the bar and fill pitcher after pitcher for big groups laughing around the tables.

To make our sangría as fresh as a customized cocktail, we macerate the fruit separately in Triple Sec and lemon juice and add it to our citrus wine blend just before serving. (The common practice of letting fruit sit in the red wine mix makes the sangría a little bitter.) Both the macerated fruit and wine mix can chill in the fridge until you're ready to dole them out, a great make-ahead party drink.

2¼ cups cut mixed fruit, such as diced apples, chopped oranges, and halved grapes

3½ fluid ounces fresh lemon juice, plus 2 ounces for marinating

2¾ fluid ounces Triple Sec, or other orange liqueur, plus 2 ounces for marinating

1 bottle (750ml) red wine, preferably a Rioja, Tempranillo, or Garnacha, or other red wine with fruit and spice notes, chilled

11 fluid ounces freshly squeezed orange juice, chilled

6 fluid ounces London dry gin, preferably Fords, chilled

8 ounces lemon-lime soda, preferably KAS Limón, chilled

Put the fruit in an airtight container. Add equal parts lemon juice and orange liqueur to barely cover it. Cover the container and refrigerate overnight.

Stir the remaining lemon juice and Triple Sec, and the wine, orange juice, and gin in a large pitcher. You can chill this mixture until you're ready to serve, for up to 24 hours.

When ready to serve, add the soda to the pitcher and stir once or twice. Drain the fruit and divide among serving glasses. Top with the chilled sangría and serve immediately.

Sangría de Piña a la Plancha (page 260)

SANGRÍA DE PIÑA A LA PLANCHA

Pineapple Sangría

Serves
8–10

Prep
30 minutes

Total
30 minutes, plus infusing overnight

1 pineapple
oil, for grilling (optional)
750ml bottle of white wine, such
    as Viura (white Rioja) or Garnacha
    Blanca
11 fluid ounces pineapple juice
5½ fluid ounces good-quality bourbon
    whiskey, such as Buffalo Trace
1 fluid ounce mezcal, such as
    Fidencio classic
4 fluid ounces Velvet Falernum
1½ fluid ounces fresh lemon juice

We serve this sangría twice a year. In January, the tropical flavor transports us from Manhattan's chilly avenues to distant warm and sandy beaches. In July and August, the savory mezcal and grilled pineapple punch is the perfect nod to the summer barbeque.

Peel the pineapple and slice it into ½-inch-thick rings. Brush a grill with a small amount of cooking oil and heat the grill to hot.

Place the rings directly on to the grill and grill on both sides until slightly charred with grill marks. Alternatively, use the broiler, first lining it with parchment paper or a nonstick silicone mat. Place the pineapple rings in the broiler for 15 minutes, until they begin to blacken/char on the outside. Remove, and let cool.

Cut each pineapple ring in half and half again to make quarters. At this point the core can be easily cut off of each piece.

Combine the liquid ingredients in a large container. Add the pineapple wedges, cover and refrigerate. Leave to infuse for at least 10 hours, or overnight.

After infusing, remove the fruit and set aside to use as garnish if desired.

PADRÓN MARGARITA

Shishito-Infused Margarita

Makes
1 drink

Prep
10 minutes

Total
10 minutes, plus infusing

Our single most popular cocktail is this spicy margarita. From the moment we created it, it became an immediate—and lasting—hit. Letting shishito peppers steep in tequila for a day gives the drink a pleasant peppery heat. We garnish the glass with a fried shishito to echo the peppery notes in the drink, but you can skip it if you want. Or, you could fry a whole batch of the peppers to nibble on while sipping your icy margarita.

---

kosher salt, for the glass
1 lime wedge
¼ cup Shishito-Infused Tequila
    (recipe follows)
2 tablespoons lime juice
1½ tablespoons Simple Syrup
    (recipe follows)
1 Pimiento de Padrón, oil patted off

Place a thin layer of salt on a saucer. Run the lime wedge against the rim of a glass, then coat the rim with salt. Use a paper towel to wipe out the inside rim so there isn't too much salt for the drink. The outside rim should still have a light coating.

Fill a cocktail shaker with ice to the rim, then add the infused tequila, lime juice, and simple syrup. Cover and shake very well, then strain into the glass. Add ice and garnish with the shishito pepper. Serve immediately.

Shishito-Infused Tequila

Makes 1 liter (approx. 1 quart)
Prep 15 minutes
Total 15 minutes, plus cooling

6 shishito peppers, split lengthwise
1 bottle (1 liter) tequila

Put the shishito peppers in the tequila. Seal with the cap and infuse for 24 hours. Strain the tequila through a fine-mesh sieve into another container with a spout. Pour back into the tequila bottle, using a funnel if you have one. The infused tequila will keep for up to 1 month.

Simple Syrup

Makes ¾ cup
Prep 5 minutes
Total 5 minutes, plus cooling

½ cup sugar

Bring the sugar and ½ cup water to a boil in a small saucepan, stirring to dissolve the sugar. Boil for 1 minute, then remove from the heat and let cool completely. The syrup can be refrigerated for up to 1 week.

Padrón Margarita (page 261)

BASES

BASES

Many Spanish home cooks still prepare a three-course meal every day. Families take advantage of a three-hour mid-afternoon break to head home for the day's principal meal. For many, this is still the cornerstone of their family life with generations of families seeing each other every day to break bread.

The task of preparing a sit-down three-course meal for several people every day may sound daunting, but Spanish home cooks have some tricks up their sleeves. Most of them prepare stocks and bases about once or twice a week and can use these in a number of different dishes.

At Boqueria, we do the same.

Our arsenal of bases includes stocks, sauces, and dressings. The ones that follow are either used more than once in this book (hello, stocks) or can be thrown onto just about anything for a little Spanish flair (we're looking at you, salsa verde).

To make the most of your bases, portion them into single-use servings and seal them in airtight containers. Label them with the name and date and refrigerate or freeze them until needed. If you have bases in the freezer, thaw them overnight in the refrigerator before cooking.

CHICKEN STOCK

Makes 10 cups
Prep 45 minutes
Total 4½ hours

Chicken bones, especially the feet, develop gelatin in stock when the cartilage melts into the simmering liquid. The resulting stock is richer than store-bought broth and is easy to make at home. Refrigerate or freeze the stock in smaller portions so you always have some on hand.

3 chicken carcasses or 2¾ pounds chicken backs, bones, wings, and necks
¼ cup blended canola-olive oil
½ large onion, cut in chunks
1 leek, cut in 3-inch lengths
1 celery stalk, sliced
1 large carrot, cut in large chunks
½ head garlic, cut through the "equator"
1 tablespoon tomato paste
2 tomatoes, cut in eighths
10 black peppercorns
10 ounces chicken feet
½ cup dry white wine

Preheat the oven to 500°F with a rimmed baking sheet on the center rack.

Place the chicken carcasses on the smoking hot baking sheet. Roast until the undersides are well browned, about 25 minutes. Flip the carcasses and roast for 5 minutes more.

Meanwhile, heat the oil in a large stockpot over medium-high heat. Add the onion, leek, celery, carrot, and garlic. Cook, stirring occasionally, until well-seared, about 10 minutes. You want the vegetables to brown well, but stay as raw as possible.

Add the tomato paste, tomatoes, and peppercorns. Cook, stirring often, until the tomatoes break down, about 5 minutes. Add the roasted chicken carcasses, chicken feet, and wine. Cook until the wine has reduced so that almost no liquid remains, about 5 minutes, then add enough cold water to cover all of the solids, about 3 quarts.

Bring to a boil over high heat, pushing in the solids to keep them submerged. Reduce the heat to low and simmer for 3 hours, skimming off any scum that rises to the surface and replenishing the water if it goes below the solids.

Strain through a fine-mesh sieve, pressing on the solids to extract as much liquid as possible. The stock can be refrigerated for up to 1 week or frozen for up to 1 month.

LOBSTER STOCK

Makes about 10 cups
Prep 1 hour
Total 2 hours

Lobster stock enriches seafood dishes with an incomparable depth. To make it, you need to follow a few simple steps. First, start with a huge pot. Next, take your time caramelizing the lobster heads to draw out their deep-sea flavor. Finally, simmer low and slow to fully infuse the stock with all the aromatics.

9 raw lobster heads (2 pounds)
½ cup extra-virgin olive oil
½ cup cooking brandy
1 large leek, white and pale green parts
   only, cut into ½-inch slices
1 carrot, peeled and cut into
   ½-inch dice
½ onion, cut into ½-inch chunks
1 head garlic, cut in half through
   its "equator"
1 celery stalk, cut into ½-inch slices
2 tablespoons sweet pimentón
   (smoked paprika)
3 tomatoes, cored and cut into
   1-inch chunks
½ cup dry white wine

Pull the top shells of the lobster heads off the bottoms. Cut the top shells in quarters and cut the bottoms in half lengthwise, then crosswise into thirds.

Heat 5 tablespoons oil in a large stockpot over high heat until smoking hot. Add the lobster pieces, in a single layer if possible. Cook, turning the pieces occasionally, until well caramelized, about 15 minutes. The shells should be bright red and the meat dark brown.

Add the brandy. If you're comfortable flambéing, light the alcohol very carefully with a long match. Otherwise, let the brandy boil until it has almost completely evaporated. Transfer the lobster pieces and all the pan juices to a large bowl.

Add the remaining 3 tablespoons oil to the same stockpot and heat over medium-high heat. Add the leek, carrot, onion, garlic, and celery. Cook, stirring occasionally, until well caramelized and browned, about 15 minutes.

Add the pimentón and stir well, then immediately add the tomatoes to prevent the pimentón from burning. Cook, stirring occasionally, until the tomatoes break down, about 3 minutes. Add the wine, bring to a boil, then simmer until reduced by half, about 1 minute. Add 4 quarts cold water and return the lobster and all its juices to the pot.

Bring to a boil over high heat, then reduce the heat to maintain a steady simmer for 30 minutes. Remove from the heat, cover, and let stand for 1 hour to steep.

Strain through a fine-mesh sieve, pressing on all the solids to extract as much liquid as possible. The stock can be refrigerated for up to 1 week or frozen for up to 6 months.

Chef's tip: You can ask for lobster heads at your local market's seafood counter. If you can't find them, use 2 pounds of large shell-on shrimp with heads instead.

VINAGRETA DE JEREZ

Makes about 1¼ cups
Prep 5 minutes
Total 5 minutes

The complex acidity of sherry vinegar—a little oaky, a little sweet—comes through in this super versatile dressing. Earthy maple syrup and the floral notes of lemon juice bind the edgy acid with fruity Spanish olive oil. Keep a jar on hand in the fridge to drizzle over any salad.

2 tablespoons maple syrup
juice of 3 lemons, about 1 cup
2 tablespoons sherry vinegar
½ cup plus 1 tablespoon extra-virgin
    olive oil
kosher salt

Whisk the syrup, lemon juice, vinegar, and oil in a bowl until smooth. Season to taste with salt and whisk well.

The vinaigrette can be refrigerated for up to 7 days.

PICKLING LIQUID

Makes about 4 cups
Prep 10 minutes
Total 10 minutes

You can pour this over anything to make pickles. Keep sliced soft vegetables like shallots and cucumbers raw and blanch hard, dense vegetables, such as cauliflower or carrots before immersing in the liquid. Seal in a jar and refrigerate for at least 1 hour and up to 1 month.

1 cup sherry vinegar
1 cup white wine vinegar
½ cup sugar
1 whole star anise
½ teaspoon black peppercorns
½ teaspoon white peppercorns
2 whole cloves
2 teaspoons yellow mustard seeds
2 guindilla peppers or chiles de árbol
1 garlic clove, peeled
1 dried bay leaf
1 small sprig of rosemary
1 sprig of thyme

Combine all of the ingredients in a medium saucepan with 2 cups water. Bring to a boil over medium heat, stirring to dissolve the sugar, then remove from the heat. Use immediately or refrigerate for up to 1 month.

Sherry Vinegar

Studies have found at least 80 unique aroma compounds in sherry vinegar. This vinegar's bright, yet rounded, signature smoky, woodsy notes result from fermenting, aging, and blending the vinegar in oak barrels.

You can find sherry vinegar in supermarkets. Look for labels with the Denominación de Origen Protegida (or DOP) seal. It means that the vinegar began as Andalusian sherry good enough to drink before spending at least six months aging. DOP Vinagre de Jerez Reserva is aged at least two years and Gran Reserva at least ten. Standard sherry vinegars tend to come from palomino grapes, while sweeter ones start with Pedro Ximénez or moscatel. We always keep a few different varieties on hand.

VINAGRETA DE CÍTRICOS

Makes about ⅔ cup
Prep 5 minutes
Total 5 minutes

This is our go-to vinaigrette with its tart duo of lemon and vinegar, softened with a little honey. It tastes great on any salad, especially ones with fruit.

2 tablespoons fresh lemon juice
1 tablespoon white wine vinegar
½ garlic clove
1 tablespoon honey
½ cup extra-virgin olive oil
kosher salt

Combine all of the ingredients with a pinch of salt in a blender and purée until very smooth. Season to taste with salt.

The vinaigrette will keep, refrigerated, for up to 5 days.

SPICED BUTTER

Makes 1½ cups
Prep 5 minutes
Total 5 minutes

This outstanding spiced butter is great served with grilled steaks (see page 211), and many other meat dishes.

1 tablespoon kosher salt
1 tablespoon freshly ground
    black pepper
1 tablespoon sweet paprika
1 tablespoon hot pimentón
    (smoked paprika)
¼ pound (1 stick) unsalted butter

Combine the salt, pepper, paprika, and pimentón in a medium bowl. Put the butter in a deep microwave-safe container and microwave in 30-second increments, until the dairy solids sink to the bottom and the clarified butter rises to the top, about 1½ minutes total. Pour the clarified butter over the spices, leaving the dairy solids behind. Stir the spiced butter well.

SOFRITO

Makes about 1 cup
Prep 30 minutes
Total 3½ hours

This saucy blend of onion, tomatoes, and garlic is the foundation of most Catalonian dishes. The very best cooks know that the longer the blend simmers, the richer it tastes. Some even leave it on the stove for a full day. We make a big batch and refrigerate or freeze the mixture in smaller ready-to-use portions, so that we can add this deep flavor to a dish in an instant.

1 pound ripe tomatoes, cut in
    1-inch chunks
1 (8-ounce) white Spanish
    onion, chopped
3 garlic cloves, peeled and trimmed
½ cup blended canola-olive oil

Put the tomatoes, onion, and garlic, in that order, into a blender or food processor. Pulse until well mixed, then purée until almost smooth but with a few small chunks remaining. Transfer to a large saucepan with the oil and stir well.

Bring to a simmer over medium heat, stirring occasionally. Reduce the heat to low and simmer, stirring occasionally, until thick and sweet, about 3 hours.

ALLIOLI

Makes 1½ cups
Prep 15 minutes
Total 15 minutes

In Catalan, allioli translates to "garlic and oil" and those are the only two ingredients in the original. It's one of the region's absolute oldest and essential sauces. Traditionally, it's made by smashing garlic in a mortar while drizzling in oil. The two emulsify to create a sauce as creamy as mayonnaise. Nailing that skill is hard, to say the least. The old-school technique may be a dying art, but the sauce itself lives on, often with a mayonnaise formula. We use a whole egg in ours to make the emulsification process easy and foolproof. It also results in an airier spread that's still luscious and garlicky.

1 large garlic clove, peeled
   and trimmed
1 large egg
¾ teaspoon white wine vinegar
¼ teaspoon Dijon mustard
1 cup blended canola-olive oil
kosher salt

Process the garlic, egg, vinegar, and mustard in a blender or food processor until smooth, scraping the bowl occasionally. With the machine running, add the oil in a very slow, steady stream. Process until emulsified, scraping the bowl occasionally. Season to taste with salt.

SPICED ALLIOLI DRESSING

Makes 1 scant cup
Prep 10 minutes
Total 10 minutes

1 garlic clove, peeled
1 large egg, at room temperature
1 teaspoon Dijon mustard
½ teaspoon sriracha
4 teaspoons white wine vinegar
¾ cup blended canola-olive oil
kosher salt

Use a zester to finely grate the garlic into a bowl. Add the egg and whisk until the egg is broken and blended. Add the mustard, sriracha sauce, and vinegar, and whisk until smooth. Continue whisking while adding the oil in a very slow, steady stream. Whisk until emulsified into a creamy dressing. Season to taste with salt.

PICADA

Makes about ⅓ cup
Prep 20 minutes
Total 20 minutes, plus overnight infusing

Mortar-and-pestle sauces are the backbone of Catalan cuisine. This pounded herb-bread paste seasons stews, paellas, and fideuas with a hit of freshness while thickening cooking liquids. Like so many Spanish staples, picada was created during tough times as an inexpensive flavor base that could enrich a wide variety of humble dishes. It still excels in doing the same now.

We make our picada a little luxurious with the addition of aromatic saffron. To streamline the step of toasting the saffron, we sprinkle it over the hot fried bread. The saffron heats up over the bread and releases its intoxicating aroma beautifully that way.

---

1 dried ñora pepper
2 garlic cloves, peeled and trimmed
½ cup flat-leaf parsley leaves
blended canola-olive oil, for frying
2 (¾-inch-thick) slices baguette
a good pinch of saffron threads
¼ cup extra-virgin olive oil
kosher salt

Cover the ñora pepper with very hot (almost boiling) water in a bowl. Let stand at room temperature overnight.

Drain the pepper and discard the stem and seeds. Use a spoon to scrape out the flesh. Reserve the flesh and discard the skin.

Put the garlic and a large pinch of salt in a mortar or food processor. Pound with a pestle or pulse the machine until the garlic becomes a paste. Add the parsley and pepper flesh and pound or pulse until the leaves are very finely ground.

Fill a small skillet with the canola-olive oil to a depth of ½ inch. Heat over medium-high heat until the oil is hot and shimmering. Add the baguette slices and cook, turning once, until golden brown and crisp on both sides. Transfer to the mortar or processor and immediately sprinkle the saffron on top. Pound or pulse until the mixture is smooth. Add the olive oil and stir with the pestle or pulse in the machine until fully incorporated.

SALSA DE AJO Y PEREJIL

Makes ⅔ cup
Prep 10 minutes
Total 10 minutes

This versatile sauce can be used to finish any grilled or sautéed vegetables, fish, or meat. In Spain, tapas bar chefs drizzle a little over everything. Home cooks sometimes just stir together chopped parsley and garlic or mix the duo with a little oil. We like the body the bread gives to the sauce, but you can leave it out if you want.

---

4 garlic cloves, peeled and halved
1 teaspoon kosher salt, plus more to taste
1 cup flat-leaf parsley leaves
2 slices Olive Oil Toast (see page 32)
½ cup extra-virgin olive oil

Pound the garlic and salt in a mortar with a pestle until the mixture is pasty and smooth. Add the parsley and pound and stir until the herbs are very finely torn. Add the toast and smash until a smooth paste forms.

Add the oil and stir until well mixed. Season to taste with salt. The salsa can be refrigerated for up to 1 week.

Chef's tip: To save time, or if your mortar is not large enough, you can pulse everything together in a food processor or blender until well mixed. Just avoid overmixing because the heat of the machine can burn the greens and oil.

SALSA VERDE

Makes about ½ cup
Prep 15 minutes
Total 15 hours

This four-herb blend includes sharp-sweet shallot and dried guindilla chili. Using both sherry vinegar and lemon juice gives a freshness and complex acidity ideal for balancing the richness of meaty dishes like Pintxos Morunos (see page 50). It's also delicious spooned over any grilled meat, fish, shellfish, or roasted vegetables.

1 packed cup finely chopped flat-leaf parsley leaves
2 tablespoons minced chives
¼ shallot, very finely chopped
1 guindilla pepper, very finely chopped or ⅛ teaspoon crushed red chili
¼ teaspoon finely chopped fresh rosemary leaves
¼ teaspoon finely chopped fresh thyme leaves
⅜ cup extra-virgin olive oil
1 teaspoon sherry vinegar
1 teaspoon lemon juice
kosher salt

Stir together the parsley, chives, shallot, pepper, rosemary, thyme, and oil in a medium bowl. Season to taste with salt. At this point, the sauce can be refrigerated for up to 3 days.

When ready to serve, stir in the vinegar and lemon juice. Season to taste with salt.

SALSA BRAVA

Makes about 4 cups
Prep 10 minutes
Total 1¼ hours

This is the sauce that makes the bravas! Tangy, thick, and smooth, this intense tomato sauce can pack a little heat or a lot, depending on how many chili peppers you throw in. It's really a matter of taste. We use dried guindilla chilies from Spain to give our sauce a little kick. If you want a fiery salsa, toss in more peppers.

Once the sauce is done, it can be served alongside allioli or mixed with it for the perfect Patatas Bravas (see page 57). If you're serving the sauces separately, you can put the brava sauce in the bottom of the dish under the potatoes, dollop onto the spuds, or serve it in a bowl on the side for dipping.

⅓ cup extra-virgin olive oil
7 garlic cloves, sliced
5 guindilla or pepperoncini peppers
½ large (minimum diameter 3 inches) white onion, thinly sliced
1 x 28-ounce can whole peeled tomatoes in sauce
½ teaspoon sugar
kosher salt and freshly ground black pepper

Combine the oil, garlic, and guindillas in a large, deep skillet. Cook over medium-high heat, stirring often, until the garlic is golden, about 2 minutes. Add the onion and season generously with salt and pepper. Cook, stirring occasionally, until the onion is very soft and caramelized, about 10 minutes.

Stir in the tomatoes, sugar, and ½ teaspoon salt. Cover, reduce the heat to medium-low, and simmer until the tomatoes lose their water, about 35 minutes.

Pass the mixture through a food mill or purée in a blender until smooth. The sauce can be refrigerated for up to 1 week. Bring to room temperature or heat before serving.

ROMESCO

Makes 3 cups
Prep 45 minutes
Total 3 hours, plus overnight soaking

Make a big batch of this Catalan sauce and you'll find yourself spooning it on everything. It's a thick, coarse olive oil blend of caramelized tomatoes, peppers, and garlic with fried bread and hazelnuts. All that richness is balanced with sherry vinegar and fresh parsley. We dip raw vegetables and crackers into it, smear it on toast and sandwiches, slather it all over grilled vegetables and fish, use it to thicken stews, and make salad dressings with it.

This recipe calls for roasting the vegetables in the oven, but in the summer, we grill them for an added smokiness. We encourage you to do the same.

---

2 dried ñora peppers
6 vine ripe tomatoes
1 head of garlic plus 1 garlic
    clove, peeled
1 cup extra-virgin olive oil, plus more
    for frying
6 (½-inch-thick) slices baguette
    (about 4 ounces)
⅔ cup hazelnuts, preferably skinned
1 cup loosely packed flat-leaf
    parsley leaves
3 tablespoons sherry vinegar
kosher salt

Place the ñora peppers in a bowl and pour very hot (almost boiling) water over them. Let stand at room temperature overnight.

Drain the peppers and discard the stem and seeds. Use a spoon to scrape out the flesh. Reserve the flesh and discard the skin.

Preheat the oven to 450°F. Line a rimmed baking tray with foil and place the tomatoes on it. Roast for 20 minutes, then place the whole head of garlic on the pan alongside the tomatoes. Continue roasting until the tomatoes are blackened and blistered and the skins on the garlic are browned, about 2 hours longer. The tomatoes should be very dry.

Meanwhile, fill a large skillet with enough oil to come ¼ inch up the sides. Heat over medium-high heat until very hot. If you touch a slice of bread to the oil, it should bubble immediately. If it doesn't, let it heat more. Add the bread in a single layer. Cook until golden brown, about 30 seconds per side. Transfer to a bowl.

Add the hazelnuts to the oil and cook, shaking the pan often, until evenly golden brown, about 1 minute. If they are already skinned, combine them with the bread. If they have skins, first transfer them to a clean kitchen towel. Wrap the nuts in the towel and rub vigorously to remove the skins. When cool enough to handle, combine them with the bread.

Remove the top ¼ inch of the head of garlic. Using your hands, squeeze the soft roasted cloves into the bread and nut mixture. Using a blender, blend the ñora pepper flesh, tomatoes, roasted garlic, raw garlic clove, fried bread, fried nuts, parsley, vinegar, and 1 cup oil until the mixture is smooth. It will be very thick and there may be some tiny bits remaining. Season to taste with salt.

The romesco can be refrigerated for up to 1 week or frozen for up to 6 weeks.

Chef's tip: Ñora peppers are available online, but you can substitute dried California (Anaheim), New Mexico, or pasilla chilies.

Ñoras

Dried ñora (or nyora) peppers are deep red, small, and circular. They're earthy and sweet, with the aroma of paprika. They should be stemmed and seeded before use and rehydrated by soaking in hot water. Once softened, the juicy flesh is scraped from the skin. You can buy ñora peppers online or from a Spanish market. If you can't find them, substitute another dried mild, sweet chili pepper, such as ancho or cascabel, a close cousin to ñora, which has the same round shape.

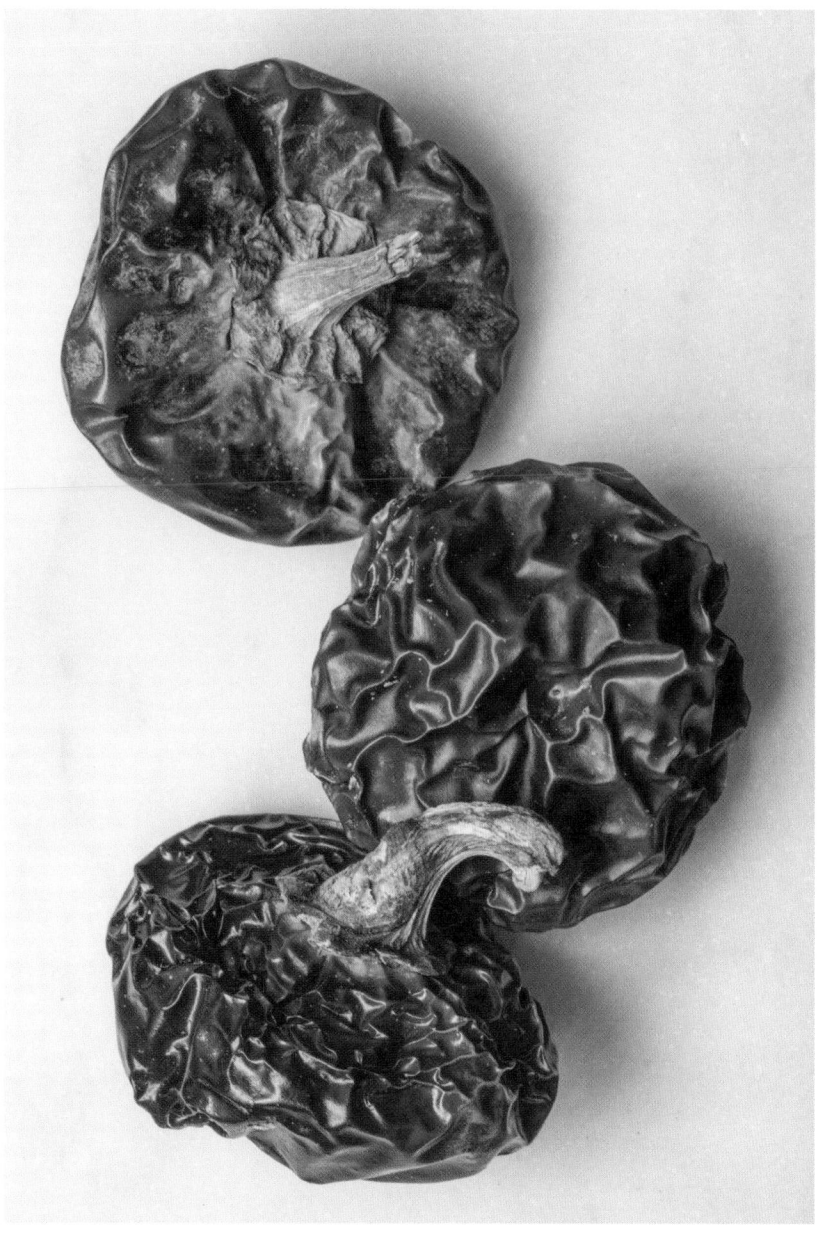

INDEX

R

S

About the Author

Zack Bezunartea started his restaurant career at 10 years old when he spent the summer after fourth grade flipping burgers at the small snack bar his parents ran in New Mexico. A short-order cook in every sense, he had to stand on a milk crate to reach the patties and top them with roasted green chile strips and slices of American cheese. He's been working in restaurants ever since.

His interest in Spanish cuisine began as a teenager when he spent a couple of summers with family in Pamplona and Bilbao. The food captured his imagination, and every day he watched with rapt attention as the afternoon meal was prepared. Notes about those meals filled half his journals from those summers where he described Basque fish stews cooked in clay pots and thin-sliced lamb chops cooked over an open fire in detail. At least two pages were dedicated to his Tia Mercedes' *croquetas*.

Back stateside he worked in restaurants during school and beyond. He was a host and a barback in Phoenix, a busboy in Portland, a server in Tucson, and a bartender in San Francisco. Eventually his love for hospitality, food, and restaurants led him into management.

As General Manager at B44, a Catalan Bistro in San Francisco's financial district, Zack finally found himself working with the Spanish food he loved so much, and he became an enthusiastic cheerleader for the still little-known cuisine, bouncing from table to table explaining the menu and making recommendations.

On a visit to New York shortly after the first Boqueria opened, Zack dropped in. He was immediately drawn in by the energy and design, and the food looked delicious too, but the wait was over an hour. He'd have to come back some other time. It would be a year before he visited again, but then he never left. He moved to New York, met with Yann and joined the opening team for Boqueria SoHo.

He loved working service at SoHo. He'd rally the troops at line-up with jokes and games, doing his best to get their energy up for the dinner rush and then dart around the dining room talking to regulars and checking in on new guests.

Today, as Director of Operations, Zack oversees the day-to-day of all the Boqueria restaurants, working alongside Managers and Chefs to make sure that every night at every Boqueria still feels the way SoHo did when he first walked in; the best party in town.

Yann's story is told on pages 12–13, and you can read all about **Marc** on pages 20–23.

Absolute Press

Bloomsbury Publishing Plc
50 Bedford Square, London, WC1B 3DP, UK

BLOOMSBURY, ABSOLUTE PRESS and the Absolute Press logo
are trademarks of Bloomsbury Publishing Plc

First published in 2018

Additional photography credits:
Page 8: Boqueria
Pages 11 and 13: Aaron Zebrook
Page 19: Francesco Bertocci - Lucy Harris Studio
Pages 186, 244, and 250: Simone Careaga

Library of Congress Cataloguing-in-Publication data has been
applied for

ISBN   HB   9781632864949
            ePub   9781632864956

2 4 6 8 10 9 7 5 3 1

Printed and bound in China by RR Donnelley Printing Solutions Ltd

Bloomsbury Publishing Plc makes every effort to ensure that the
papers used in the manufacture of our books are natural, recyclable
products made from wood grown in well-managed forests. Our
manufacturing processes conform to the environmental regulations
of the country of origin.

To find out more about our authors and books visit www.bloomsbury.
com and sign up for our newsletters

Credits

Publisher Jon Croft
Commissioning Editor Meg Avent
Project Editors Emily North and Callie Garnett
Project Director Simone Careaga
Designer Marie O'Mara
Junior Designer Nathan Shellard
Photographer James Pomerantz
Illustrator Magpie Studio
Food and Prop Stylist Mariana Velasquez
Editor Eleanor Van Zandt
Home Economists Rachael Daylong and Loren Wood
Proofreader and Indexer Zoë Ross